THE FOUR GOSPEL
ESOTERICALLY
INTERPRETED

(1937)

ILLUMINATING RENDITION OF THE HIDDEN, ESOTERIC MEANING OF THE GOSPELS.

John P. Scott

ISBN 1-56459-804-7

Kessinger Publishing's Rare Reprints
Thousands of Scarce and Hard-to-Find Books!

-
-
-
-
-
-
-
-
-
-
-
-
-
-
-
-
-
-
-
-
-
-

We kindly invite you to view our extensive catalog list at:
http://www.kessinger.net

An Acknowledgment

WE WISH to express our deepest gratitude to many people for their assistance in making it possible for the esoteric information in this and the other books and booklets by the writer to reach the public.

First, acknowledgment is due my dear wife, Dorothy Louise Scott, for long hours of patient toil in typing and correcting grammatically many, many manuscripts.

Second, my friend, Howard A. Burk, who has printed the writer's previous books and booklets without profit to himself.

Third, other pioneers in the esoteric Bible field, especially Max Heindel, Elijah Brookshire, Corinne Dunklee, James Pryse, Dr. George Carey and others.

Will the reader, if he has gained some added light from this volume, remember these lovely souls in his meditation, and return to them some of the love which they so freely gave out to others.

The Gospel According to
ST. MATTHEW

CHAPTER 1.

"The book of the generation of Jesus Christ, the son of Abraham. Abraham begat Isaac; and Isaac begat Jacob; and Jacob begat Judas and his brethren".

The names comprising the genealogy of Jesus at the beginning of St. Matthew tell esoterically the evolution of mankind from the time we left the heaven worlds to begin our descent into matter, until each of us shall reach great spiritual illumination through bringing about the alchemical marriage of the head and the heart.

Abraham, the first of the line, means "the father of a multitude". Thus we start with a "multitude" of virgin spirits coming from the Father and descending from the heaven worlds or the "Garden of Eden" into material conditions. This is the same story as that of Adam and Eve, since this symbolic couple represent the masculine and feminine of all humanity.

Isaac means "joy and laughter". In those early days infant humanity were perfectly happy before they had descended into a more materialistic world.

Isaac begat Jacob, "the supplanter", and this ideal condition was "supplanted" by one not so happy.

Jacob begat Judas, whose name is interpreted as "praised" and which tells us that early humanity worshipped or praised God even after the first conditions were changed or "supplanted".

"And Judas begat Phares and Zara of Thamar; and Phares begat Esrom; and Esrom begat Aram;"

Phares means "breach" or "break". This clearly symbolizes that period when our ancient ancestors ate of the "Tree of Knowledge", causing the "break" or change in our early history known as the expulsion of Adam and Eve from the "Garden of Eden".

The mother of Zara ("sunrise") and of Phares ("breach") was Thamar, which means "a palm tree". Because of the fact that the palm tree has both the masculine and feminine sexes, we believe this indicates that the "break" in the normal course of evolution took place when the Sun rose or shone clearly for the first time upon the ancient continent of Atlantis, shortly after the division of humanity into separate sexes. (There was a time when we were dual-sexed). The palm tree also symbolizes fertility, and it was after this division into separate sexes that primitive mankind took to themselves the unrestrained use of the generative function.

From Phares came Esrom, which means "a dwelling". Thus, we are told that primitive mankind began to build dense bodies or "dwelling houses" for the Spirit. These bodies were possessed of both the masculine and the feminine attributes of sex, as shown by the fact that Esrom begat Aram, which means "certain districts in Syria and Mesopotamia". Mesopotamia means, "the country of the two rivers". Syria was a country along the eastern coast of the Mediterranean, extending inland to Mesopotamia. The capital of Syria was Damascus, called "the most ancient city in the world". A "city" symbolizes a state of consciousness. If the reader will put two and two together he will see that the "country of the two rivers" in the "eastern" part or front of the body, has to do with the positive and negative, or masculine and feminine, polarities of sex, located in that region of the body. Damascus, the capital, being the oldest "city" (state of consciousness) in the "world", tells us that physical or sex consciousness was the "oldest" or first consciousness possessed by mankind after descending from the heaven worlds into denser matter. Consequently, in one word, Aram, we are told that the first consciousness of primitive man was sexual, brought about by the development of the two separate sex manifestations.

"And Aram begat Aminadab; and Aminadab begat Naasson; and Naasson begat Salmon;"

Aminadab means "kin of princes", which explains the fact that at one time in its early development mankind received assistance from certain spiritual hierarchies, here described as "princes", in learning to evolve. Mankind was "kin" to these spiritual Beings since all of us are Children of God, and as such are naturally related to each other, although each class belongs to a different stage in evolution.

Aminadab begat Naasson, meaning "alchemist". As a result of this assistance from spiritual hierarchies, mankind begins to develop into alchemists, or begins to turn the base metals of the being into spiritual "gold". In another sense, the "Prodigal Son" had begun the return journey to the Father. Salmon "a garment", comes next. As a result of the practice of this divine alchemy, humanity begins to weave the "soma psuchicon" or the "golden wedding garment" (also known as "King Solomon's Temple" in Masonry), in which we shall meet the Christ at His second coming.

"And Salmon begat Booz of Rachab; and Booz begat Obed of Ruth; and Obed begat Jesse".

Booz symbolizes "strength", and when we have built the "golden wedding garment", we will have at our command the spiritual strength generated through that vehicle. It is said that Booz was the son of Rachab, a harlot. This tells us that the feminine principle or the Life Force, so often used in sensual gratification (as a "harlot"), when conserved and used for regeneration, gives strength to the individual. The next name is Obed, meaning "to worship". When we have lived the story told by the previous names, we will then begin to truly worship God. Obed was the son of Ruth, which means "a friend". Ruth also represents the feminine force, which is a "friend" to mankind when used constructively for regeneration.

Obed produced Jesse, whose spiritual significance is "a gift." When we have produced "Jesse" within ourselves, we will make a gift of all that we are and have to God, in the service of humanity.

"And Jesse begat David the king; and David the king begat Solomon of her that had been the wife of Urias;"

The next step after dedicating our lives in unselfish service is to become "David". This name means "beloved of God". We will then be both "kings" and "priests", excelling along both physical and spiritual lines. We will be high Initiates and will soon produce "Solomon" within ourselves. The esoteric meaning of Solomon is "peace and wisdom". Solomon's mother, Bath-sheba, was the "daughter of the oath", which explains that peace and wisdom will come to us only after we have taken a pledge or an oath that the lower phase of our being must serve the higher.

It is the belief of the writer that this first half of the geneology shows the development of the mystic or heart side of humanity. The second half indicates the development of the occult or mental side. In other words, the esoteric meaning of the characters from Abraham to Solomon explains the raising of the Life Force through the heart, which produces mystical illumination. The second half of the names explains the raising of this Force directly up the spinal cord to the head.

Having briefly interpreted the concealed message explaining mystic development, we will now see what steps are required for the occultist. (The reader will note that the names used in the Book of Ruth are very similar to the names just interpreted). The New Testament, however, goes a step farther than the Old in showing both head and heart development, and also Adeptship, which is the balance of the two.

"And Solomon begat Roboam; and Roboam begat Abia; and Abia begat Asa;"

Solomon (the wisdom principle) produces Roboam, which means "who enlarges the people". "People" symbolizes the ordinary mass consciousness. Thus, when we acquire wisdom, our normal consciousness becomes enlarged or expands.

Next comes Abia, which means "following". He in turn produces Asa, which signifies "physician". The story told by these two names is that "following" this "expansion of consciousness", humanity begins to heal itself or to become its own spiritual physician. The healing is naturally from the disastrous effects of the misuse of the creative function, from which we all suffer today. Then humanity begins to learn something of the Mosaic Law of Cause and Effect. This is shown by the next name, Josaphat.

"And Asa begat Josaphat; and Josaphat begat Joram; and Joram begat Ozias;"

Josaphat means "Jehovah judges". Humanity begins to realize the justness of the Jehovistic or Mosaic Law of Cause and Effect and the opportunity to work out karma thereby. They exalt Jehovah for His just laws. Joram means "Jehovah is exalted".

The symbolism of Ozias is "Jehovah (or God) is my strength," showing that humanity must realize that their strength is not in themselves but in God.

"And Ozias begat Joatham; and Joatham begat Achaz; and Achaz begat Ezekias;"

Joatham has the meaning, "God is perfect", and symbolizes the dawning consciousness of humanity concerning the perfection of God. Close study will easily convince the reader that these are indeed steps in the spiritualization of the occult or mental type. Achaz and Ezekias represent respectively, "he hath seized" and "God hath strengthened." The person who accepts God, or whom the Spirit has "seized" or accepted, becomes "strengthened".

"And Ezekias begat Manasses; and Manasses begat Amon; and Amon begat Josias;"

Manasses means "one who causes to forget". This tells us that humanity is beginning to forget its former misery caused by disobedience to God's laws. The next two names, Amon, "master workman", and Josias, "God supports", symbolize the fact that the mind (which is the "master workman"), assisted or "supported" by God, is steadily building the occult path. Manasses may also have another meaning, for shortly after the period in Jewish history indicated by Manasses the Jews were carried away into Babylon. Therefore, this might also symbolize the slipping back of the mind at times into a lower state of consciousness. In any event, however, the mind is the "master workman", and when supported or spiritualized by God, it lifts us back into the higher consciousness.

It is stressed, both in the development of the heart and of the mind, that there are times when we yield to the temptations of Lucifer. We are "carried away into Babylon" or materiality. This is expressed in the life of Jesus as the "flight into Egypt" or "darkness". It will be noted that the flight into Egypt was made when Jesus was only a child and not after He had gained and proven His spiritual strength. From these falls into sin we gain much valuable experience which helps to prevent their recurrence.

"And Josias begat Jechonias and his brethren, about the time they were carried away to Babylon: And after they were brought to Babylon, Jechonias begat Salathiel; and Salathiel begat Zorobabel; and Zorobabel begat Abiud; and Abiud begat Eliakim; and Eliakim begat Azor;"

Jechonias, who was carried away into Babylon, means "God establishes". The mind may yield to temptation, but when it attains to the higher consciousness again, Salathiel, "I ask God", appears on the scene. This reveals that after the fall of the mind we "ask God" the reason for the temptation, in order that the mind may not yield a second time. Consequently, by "asking God" (Salathiel), "God establishes" (Jechonias) or makes our foundations sure.

Zorobabel means "begotten in Babylon", and naturally indicates the added experience which the mind gains during its "captivity" in this lower state of consciousness. As a result, a greater understanding of the majesty of God is born, symbolized by Abiud. (Abiud means "my father is majesty"). Humanity then becomes more firmly "established" in evolution, as represented by the name Eliakim. This is done with the aid of great spiritual Beings. A hint of their help is given in the name Azor, which means "helper".

"And Azor begat Sadoc; and Sadoc begat Achim;' and Achim begat Eliud;"

Sadoc means "righteousness", and as a result of our righteousness, Achim is produced. Achim has the same meaning as Jachin. Jachin is the second pillar of the "Temple of Solomon". Booz or Boaz is the other pillar. These two pillars represent the two paths taken by the ascending Spinal Spirit Fire in the regeneration of the body. We are now at the same point in our story on the occult path as we were when the name Booz appeared previously, but then the mystical path was being given. This point is the arrival of the Spinal Spirit dicated its arrival at the top of the heart pillar. Now we have its arrival at the top of the path or "pillar" used by the occultist.

"And Eliud begat Eleazar; and Eleazar begat Matthan; and Matthan begat Jacob; And Jacob begat Joseph the husband of Mary, of whom was born Jesus, who is called Christ."

The five names above symbolize the following: Eliud, "God of Judah"; Eleazar, "God has aided"; Mattan, "a gift"; Jacob "supplanter"; and Joseph, "the budding rod". Collectively, they mean that the "God of Judah" aids humanity to make a "gift" of itself to God, which process results in the "budding rod" or the raising of the Life Force up the spinal cord to the brain. "Joseph", the spiritualized mind, then unites with "Mary", the pure heart, which produces the "Jesus" within. This is the "Son" or "Christ Child" produced by the union of the spiritualized head and heart. This "Son" is christened or "Christed" with the power of God, which descends as a dove.

CHAPTER 2.

"Now when Jesus was born in Bethlehem of Judaea in the days of Herod the king, behold, there came wise men from the east to Jerusalem. Saying, Where is he that is born King of the Jews? for we have seen his star in the east, and are come to worship him".

The three wise men represent the three extra pairs of nerves in the sacral region of the body, which the neophyte will spiritualize in time. When these three "wise men" or nerves "follow the star" up to "Bethlehem" (in the body), we will become attuned to the solar instead of the lunar month. We will need less food and less sleep and will possess much more personal power. The "gifts" of the "three wise men" are not something imaginary, but are very real and very wonderful. The "east" represents the lower region of the body. Bethlehem ("house of bread") symbolizes the solar plexus or "manger" of the body.

"When Herod the king had heard these things, he was troubled, and all Jerusalem with him. And when he had gathered all the chief priests and scribes of the people together, he demanded of them where Christ should be born".

Herod is, of course, the lower nature. At the beginning of our story the lower nature has strong control of the neophyte. He is naturally troubled at any spiritual advancement in the neophyte and wishes to destroy it. This lower self seeks more information from the faculties (chief priests and scribes) that it may more easily destroy this new spiritual quality. It knows that the birth of the Christ Consciousness will be its undoing if it does not destroy it before it attains to maturity and power.

"And they said unto him, In Bethlehem of Judaea: for thus it is written by the prophet, And thou Bethlehem in the land of Juda, art not the least among the princes of Juda: for out of thee shall come a Governor, that shall rule my people Israel".

"My people Israel" represents those parts of the being, or that consciousness, that is constructive. It is a well-known teaching of occultism that the life of Jesus Christ is re-enacted both physiologically and spiritually within the being of the neophyte. Therefore, that "Jesus" principle born in the "manger" of the body will in time grow and ascend and ultimately rule all of the constructive phases of the being.

"Then Herod, when he had privily called the wise men, enquired of them diligently what time the star appeared."

"And he sent them to Bethlehem, and said, Go and search diligently for the young child: and when ye have found him, bring me word again, that I may come and worship him also".

This "star" is something that must be formed by the neophyte himself, and must lead the "wise men" with their precious gifts from "east" to "west". Yet it is also true that "Herod" sends the "wise men" to "Bethlehem", since the force that carries them is the same force that gives "Herod" life and being. The only thought of the lower nature is treachery. Nevertheless, it does assist in the process of regeneration.

"When they had heard the king, they departed, and lo the star, which they saw in the east, went before them, till it came and stood over where the young child was. When they saw the star, they rejoiced with exceeding great joy".

The departure of the "wise men" from "Herod" and the lower region and their "following the star" is a physiological process. This star takes them to that place in the body where occult teachers say, a spiritual impulse is born each time the Moon makes her circuit. All Cosmic events are shown by the movement of the heavenly bodies, and "As above so below". Naturally then, the stars must indicate to the neophyte when the time is right for the spiritual birth within his own being. Of course, there is exceeding great joy when the added force of the "wise men" is brought into activity within the "temple" or the body.

"And when they were come into the house, they saw the

young child with Mary his mother, and fell down and worshipped him: and when they had opened their treasures, they presented unto him gifts; gold, and frankincense and myrrh".

The gifts brought by the wise men represent added forces or qualities which are produced as a result of the spiritualization of the three extra pair of nerves. The first gift "gold", represents Wisdom, and it requires no stretch of the imagination for us to see that we will have much more wisdom when we have used the Life Force to spiritualize this extra pair of nerves. The second gift is "frankincense". Frankincense means "the oil of life". For those who wish to know more concerning this "oil" and its working in the body, we suggest a study of "Revelation, Esoterically Interpreted" by the author. On Page 20 of this book a physiological statement by a former professor at Cornell explains in detail the working and results of the "oil of life" in the body. The next gift is "myrrh". Myrrh represents Purity. Symbolically, the activity of the "three wise men" is another way of expressing regeneration, and this naturally brings the gift of Purity.

"And being warned of God in a dream that they should not return to Herod, they departed into their own country another way. And when they were departed, behold, the angel of the Lord appeareth to Joseph in a dream, saying, Arise, and take the young child and his mother and flee into Egypt and be thou there until I bring thee word: for Herod will seek this young child to destroy him. When he arose, he took the young child and his mother by night and departed into Egypt: And was there until the death of Herod: that it might be fulfilled which was spoken of the Lord by the prophet, saying, Out of Egypt have I called my son".

We believe that those who "follow the star" in higher occult exercises as given by the Rosicrucian Fellowship know that the "wise men" returned home only after a very long journey. We are not at liberty to explain in detail exactly what Verse 12 means to us. We earnestly recommend, however, the works of Max Heindel and the curriculum of the Rosicrucian Fellowship of Oceanside, California.

The flight of the young child into Egypt indicates the slipping back of the neophyte into his former condition of darkness. This happens not once but many times in our careers and continues to happen until "Herod" or the lower nature is no longer alive within us. We are all in spiritual "darkness" until the "Christ Child" becomes old enough and strong enough to lead us to the light. "Out of Egypt have I called my son", the verse says. It is true that the God Within must call each of us out of our spiritual darkness into the light of understanding and illumination.

"Then Herod, when he saw that he was mocked of the wise men, was exceeding wroth, and sent forth, and slew all the children that were in Bethlehem and in all the coasts thereof, from two years old and under, according to the time which he had diligently enquired of the wise men".

It is said to require about three and a half years to complete the process of regeneration physiologically. That is perhaps why "Herod" only slays "children" up to the age of two years. After this point the spiritual "children" or impulses have grown too strong for him to destroy easily. The reason "Herod" destroys "children" is that they are the product of the heart or emotional nature, and naturally the lower self tries to use all of the force of the emotions in a sensual way.

"Then was fulfilled that which was spoken by Jeremy the prophet, saying, In Rama was there a voice heard, lamentation, and weeping for her children, and would not be comforted, because they are not."

Does not the "Rachel" or higher emotional self within each of us cry after we have yielded to the lower nature and allowed "Herod" to misuse or "kill" our emotional forces or "children" through gratification of the lower desires? This wasting of the Life Force brings nothing but pain and sorrow to the feminine pole of being. There can be no real progress on the occult path while "Herod" is allowed to kill these "children".

"But when Herod was dead, behold an angel of the Lord appeareth in a dream to Joseph in Egypt. Saying, arise, and take the young child and his mother and go into the land of Israel: for they are dead which sought the young child's life."

Joseph represents the head and Mary the heart. When the mind realizes that the lower nature is dead or has been conquered, he knows that he can then bring the "young child" out of Egypt. It is a distinct and definite step in the life of the neophyte when "Herod" dies within him. There are very few occult students who reach this point in one life. From then on real progress is made, and without the constant battle with the lower nature. The growing Christ Consciousness is an ever-increasing aid on the Path. It may be digressing, but the writer would like to say that a careful perusal of that section of the Rosicrucian Cosmo-Conception devoted to nutrition will help to bring about the death of "Herod" more quickly and safely than ordinarily is possible. We also recommend the work of Prof. Arnold Ehret, T. de La Torre and Dr. Walter Seigmeister as being helpful in conquering the lower nature through diet.

"And he arose, and took the young child and his mother,

and came into the land of Israel, but when he heard that Archelaus did reign in Judaea in the room of his father Herod, he was afraid to go thither: notwithstanding being warned of God in a dream, he turned aside into the parts of Galilee. And he came and dwelt in a city called Nazareth; that it might be fulfilled which was spoken by the prophets, He shall be called a Nazarene."

These last verses of Chapter 2 tell us that the spiritual force in regeneration is not brought directly into 'Jerusalem' or the head. There is a process that must take place in which the force is raised little by little. Galilee was looked down upon by many people of that time. Thus, the Christ principle must dwell in and spiritualize the humble phases of our being before it can be brought or raised to "Jerusalem", as this final step produces an enlightened consciousness or illumination.

CHAPTER 3

"In those days came John the Baptist, preaching in the wilderness of Judaea: And saying; Repent ye, for the kingdom of heaven is at hand. For this is he that was spoken of by the prophet Esaias, saying, The voice of one crying in the wilderness, Prepare ye the way of the Lord, make his path straight."

John the Baptist represents the mind or mental enlightenment. That is why it is said that John the Baptist must come first. It is necessary for us to have some understanding concerning regeneration before we can intelligently proceed. We must first become awakened through our mental faculties to the necessity of purifying the body before we raise the Christ Force. This "John" preaches to the various faculties in the unregenerated body or "wilderness" that they must make of this "wilderness" a kingdom of heaven. John tells us that we must "prepare the way of the Lord" (the ways taken by the Christ Force) and "make his path straight." We must first properly purify our bodies and then direct the Life Force up the straight path of regeneration. This process is taught in the Rosicrucian Fellowship to its esoteric students.

"And the same John had his raiment of camel's hair, and a leathern girdle about his loins; and his meat was locusts and wild honey."

The "raiment of camel's hair" appears to signify the vehicle of an Initiate; while the "leathern girdle" around his loins reveals the fact that his generative faculty (the region of the loins) was "girded" or restrained. This shows that he had spiritualized his body through control of the lower nature. Each of us must pass through the same process and wear the "leathern girdle" of self-restraint. Locusts describe the

Life Force. We all know how very destructive locusts can be. However, this same force can be changed from a destructive to a constructive one. That is why it is said that John's meat was "locusts". Instead of allowing the "locusts" or Life Force to be destructive through sensual gratification, John directed this Force upward in regeneration and caused it to illumine or "feed" him both physically and spiritually. "Wild honey" is also descriptive of the assimilation of this conquered animal force. When used as a spiritual power it is very "sweet", in a spiritual sense.

"Then went out to him Jerusalem, and all Judaea, and all the region round about Jordan. And were baptized of him in Jordan, confessing their sins."

The above verses show how, through mental enlightenment, we can "baptize" or cleanse all parts of our being with the mystic "water" or force of the "River Jordan". The "River Jordan" is the Life Force ascending the spinal canal. It is through the conservation and direction of this Force that we are "washed clean" of our many sins. This is not done, however, without the cleansing blood of Christ. Without Christ we could do nothing. It is the Christ Within that directs the force of the "River Jordan" in cleansing and illumining our beings.

"But when he saw many of the Pharisees and Sadducees come to his baptism, he said unto them, O generation of vipers, who hath warned you to flee from the wrath to come? Bring forth therefore fruits meet for repentance: And think not to say within yourselves, We have Abraham to our father: for I say unto you that God is able of these stones to raise up children unto Abraham. And now also the axe is laid unto the root of the trees: therefore every tree which bringeth not forth good fruit is hewn down, and cast into the fire."

The "wrath to come" clearly indicates the Law of Karma or the Law of Cause and Effect, which the occult student knows so well. We realize that we must pay in time for the evil we have done in the past. John asks the Pharisees and the Sadducees who has told them of the Law of Cause and Effect that they should come to him for help. He explains that there is no evasion of their karmic debts, but that they must bring forth "fruits meet for repentance" or, in other words, they must perform benevolent, constructive acts that will balance or pay their evil deeds. For an illustration of the working of this Law, told in interesting narrative form, read "Magnificent Obsession" by Lloyd Douglas. This will give the reader many hints as to how he may work with the Law in order to achieve a most successful life in every way.

John clearly states a truth concealed beneath the literal

messages to the Pharisees and Sadducees. This truth is that only the spiritual attributes of the being and those capable of spiritualization will endure; all others must be burned away in the fire of purification, or "cut away" by the spiritual "axe" which takes away all that is not enduring from the "Tree of Life."

The statement that we cannot count on our divine origin, but must show that divine origin in our lives, is worth considering. The Rosicrucian Philosophy teaches us that our bodies were once mineral-like. Therefore, it is indeed true that God is able of the very stones to raise up children unto Abraham. In fact, the "stones" (the mineral kingdom) are the manifestation of a "younger" group of spirits who will some day have human bodies and who are just as much the "sons of Abraham" as we are. God is indeed "able of these stones to raise up children unto Abraham." Unless we continue to progress and develop, these younger spirits will pass us in the Race. This is one of the truths which John gave out esoterically for the benefit of those who possessed sufficient spiritual awakening to understand.

"I indeed baptize you with water unto repentance: but he that cometh after me is mightier than I, whose shoes I am not worthy to bear: he shall baptize you with the Holy Ghost, and with fire: Whose fan is in his hand, and he will throughly purge his floor, and gather his wheat into the garner; but he will burn up the chaff with unquenchable fire."

John represents the mind or mental enlightenment. The spiritual mind is able to conserve the "water of life" and "baptize" the faculties of the body with this conserved force. However, the one to come after him (the purified heart or love principle, as symbolized by Jesus Christ) is capable of bringing down the power of the Holy Ghost in a spiritual baptism--the fire of the spiritual down-pouring. In the allegory above John emphasizes the fact that the pure heart is more to be desired even than the enlightened mind. The pure heart is able to "thoroughly purge his floor" or to cleanse the being, gathering and saving all of the good attributes, but "burning" (in the fire of conscience and remorse) the bad. The reason John says that he is unworthy to bear the shoes of Jesus, who represents the purified heart, is this: Shoes symbolize the outward or most material part of a thing. The mind, therefore, admits that it is not as worthy as even the most outward phase of the purified heart.

"Then cometh Jesus from Galilee to Jordan unto John, to be baptized of him. But John forbad him saying, I have need to be baptized of thee, and comest thou to me? And Jesus answering said unto him, Suffer it to be so now: for thus it becometh us to fulfill all righteousness. Then he suffered him."

It appears universally agreed among Bible interpreters that the River Jordan represents the "river" which flows along the spinal canal. The coming of Jesus to John to be baptized symbolizes, in one sense, the fact that the heart allows the mind to direct the "water of life" up this spinal canal to the heart. In this process the heart is thoroughly washed in this spiritual stream. Each of us must in time raise this Force to the heart. This is known as the mystic path, to distinguish it from the path of the occultist. The occultist raises this "river of life" directly up the spinal canal to the brain. It is needless to say that the method of the occultist is the far more dangerous path in every way. In the Rosicrucian work, as given to its deeper students, this process is carried on in such a way that a rounded, complete development results, without danger to the student.

"And Jesus, when he was baptized, went up straightway out of the water: and lo, the heavens were opened unto him, and he saw the Spirit of God descending like a dove, and lighting upon him: And lo a voice from heaven, saying, This is my beloved Son, in whom I am well pleased."

In the above two verses we have a description of one of the beautiful steps along the ascending path of the mystic. When the force from the "river of life" "baptizes" or floods the heart of the pure mystic, it takes him straight out of his body. He becomes a "son of God" in a truer sense than ever before, since his personality has bcome completely submerged in the Christ Consciousness. From the historical angle, we are told that when John baptized Jesus, Jesus left the body and the great Cosmic Christ took possession of it and used it as a vehicle through which He might manifest to humanity. Christ left the body of Jesus when the body was crucified upon the cross, after saying, "Consummatum Est", indicating that His work was finished. At the time of the baptism the Ego known as Jesus ascended into the heaven worlds and heard the voice which said, "This is my beloved Son."

When we become pure enough to achieve this liberation from the cramping body, the personality will turn the body over to the Christ Within, which will henceforth be the ruler of our beings. This Christ Within will assist us in attaining to the ability to enter and leave the body at will. If the reader will carefully study the pledge taken in many orthodox churches by the church member at baptism, he will see that this is a very serious occasion. Baptism represents the raising of the individual above the "waters" of generation. Therefore, even in our churches, the aspirant to baptism takes a pledge of purity. In the Rosicrucian Fellowship the Probationer-to-be realizes more fully what this pledge means. He promises that the lower self will serve the higher in the service of humanity. During the taking of this pledge, he is over-shadowed by a higher Being. The reader may see by this how the great events in the life of Jesus, the Christ, are patterns which clearly indicate steps to be taken by each neophyte at the proper time.

CHAPTER 4

"Then was Jesus led up of the spirit in the wilderness to be tempted of the devil. And when he had fasted forty days and nights he was afterward an hungered. And when the tempter came to him, he said, If thou be the Son of God, command that these stones be made bread. But he answered and said, It is written, Man shall not live by bread alone, but by every word that proceedeth out of the mouth of God."

Wilderness always symbolizes a place of preparation. We will remember that the children of Israel stayed forty years in the wilderness before they could enter the "Promised Land." A wilderness is a place without the comforts and allurements of civilization. It indicates a place where the strictest discipline is practiced. We understand, therefore, that the body of Jesus, now used by the Christ, was put through a period of severe discipline. Each of us, when we have turned over our bodies to the Christ Consciousness, must go through a period of this same discipline. The stay in the wilderness was for forty days and forty nights. "40" represents, symbolically, the time necessary for preparation. Remember that the Ark floated above the Flood for forty days. This is somewhat the same story but told in different symbolism.

It might be well to note that Jesus Christ, Elijah, Moses, David and many of the other ancient characters went through this period of forty-day fasting as a means of purification and preparation. The disciples of Pythagoras who were admitted into the higher degrees of Initiation were also required to fast for forty days before taking the most advanced spiritual steps.

After Jesus Christ had accomplished his forty-day fast, the "Tempter" was met and easily discomfited. Let the neophyte who possesses many bad habits that he wishes to overcome take note. Although it is not wise to fast beyond one's capacity, nevertheless, at some time we must follow the lives of these great Bible characters. When the Disciples were not able to cast out certain of the most stubborn kind of devils, Christ tells them, "These kind come not out except through fasting and prayer." Meditate carefully (since we must live this story ourselves), that it was AFTER the fast that the "Tempter" was met and overcome.

The first temptation of Christ was a physical or a material one. This is the lowest or first of the temptations which the neophyte must eventually conquer, the physical appetites and material conditions. It is indeed true that at a later date Man shall not live as much by physical bread as he shall by the WORD or power which proceeds from God. The writer believes that he will take this in through the head instead of through the spleen, as is being done at present during sleep at night. Then, also, it will be the direct rays of the Sun which he will absorb, instead of the reflected rays from the Moon through which we are re-vitalized during the night at the present time. As explained previously, he will also have attuned himself to the solar instead of the lunar month. Many other great changes are in store for us also. We will eat less of physical food and live more by the "Word of God". (The Brothers of the Rose Cross eat physical food only in periods measured by years).

"Then the devil taketh him up into the holy city, and setteth him on a pinnacle of the temple. And saith unto him. If thou be the Son of God, cast thyself down: for it is written, He shall give his angels charge concerning thee, and in their hands they shall bear thee up, lest at any time thou dash thy foot against a stone. Jesus said unto him: It is written again, Thou shalt not tempt the Lord thy God."

As the first temptation of Christ was a physical one, so this second temptation had to do with the mind. The first temptation was that Christ use His powers to make bread in order to satisfy His hunger. This might also symbolize any other physical thing which might be desirable, such as wealth, personal power, etc. The second temptation was that he misuse the power of His mind. Kindly remember, dear reader, that these are symbolic of tests that we ourselves must pass successfully some day. The pinnacle of the temple represents the head, and Christ is asked by Satan to center His consciousness on evil or low things in order to test whether or not His powers are sufficient to protect Him from harm. The lowering of one's consciousness is what is meant by "casting one's self down from the pinnacle of the temple." Christ declines to test His spiritual power of mind needlessly by descending to a lower level. He warns Satan to cease tempting the higher nature, the God Within. As a quality in a story which must be enacted within each of us, Satan naturally symbolizes the lower nature, which endeavors to tempt the spiritualized mind or consciousness to become aware of low things or thoughts.

Again, the devil taketh him up into an exceeding high mountain, and sheweth him all the kingdoms of the world, and the glory of them; And saith unto him, All these things will I give thee, if thou wilt fall down and worship me. Then saith Jesus unto him, Get thee hence, Satan; for it is written, Thou shalt worship the Lord thy God, and him only shalt thou serve. Then the devil leaveth him and behold angels came and ministered unto him."

This "exceeding high mountain" represents a very high spiritual plane of consciousness. From such a vantage point, Christ is able to see both past, present and future and all of the splendor of many worlds. He realizes that He may choose, if He wishes, to relinquish the lowly life of Jesus of Nazareth and avoid the terrible persecution and crucifixion which must be His lot. Instead, He is free to remain in the heaven worlds and enjoy the great spiritual beauty and perfect peace that prevails there. In a lesser degree, we, as neophytes on the occult path, will also have the same decision to make: whether we will do the work that brings persecution and disgrace or whether we will enjoy the plaudits and honors of the world, but leaving a necessary though disagreeable job undone.

Christ drives the devil from Him and chooses to descend to the lower plane on which humanity dwells, where He will suffer and die for an ungrateful people. He submerges His own will and desire in the will of the Father, for loving, self-forgetting service, that a great work may be done. This, of course, attracts the ministering love of the angels, which symbolizes the fact that the being of anyone making such a sacrifice is blessed by a down-pouring of spiritual force.

"Now when Jesus had heard that John was cast into prison, he departed into Galilee. And leaving Nazareth, he came and dwelt in Capernaum, which is upon the sea coast, in the borders of Zabulon and Nepthalim: That it might be fulfilled which was spoken by Esaias the prophet, saying, The land of Zabulon and the land of Nepthalim, by the way of the sea, beyond Jordan, Galilee of the Gentiles. The people which sat in darkness saw great light; and to them which sat in the region and shadow of death light is sprung up."

The casting of John into prison may be taken two ways. The body is the "prison house" of the Spirit. John's being cast into prison might indicate a mind that was firmly seated in the body or which could not be shaken, or it could denote a mind turning materialistic. The present intent appears to be to show that the mind or "John" was firmly anchored. With the mind firmly set, the "Christ", or that force in the body, proceeds to visit various "cities" or parts of the body that have not been previously spiritualized. Capernaum is on the northwest shore of the Sea of Galilee, which indicates that this Life Force or Christ Force is being raised in the body (West and north both indicate the higher parts of the body, just as south and east indicate the lower parts). This is a process which the neophyte himself must go through when he reaches this advanced stage on the Path.

Capernaum means "consolation"; Zabulon means "an elevation"; and Nephthalim means "my wrestling." The writer, therefore, takes the names of these cities visited by Christ to indicate esoterically that through effort (wrestling) the Christ Within has ascended higher in the body (elevation) and the neophyte is well-pleased or "consoled" at the work.

The sentence, "The people which sat in darkness saw great light", means that those faculties which were formerly dormant were made spiritually active or enlightened as a result of being "visited" by this Christ Force. Also, the sentence, "And to them which sat in the region and shadow of death light is sprung up," reveals that those faculties which were dead to the things of the Spirit now become spiritually active.

"From that time Jesus began to preach and to say, Repent: for the kingdom of heaven is at hand."

When the Christ Spirit begins to "preach" in the body, it is indeed true that the kingdom of heaven is close at hand. As He states, "The kingdom of heaven is within," and the previous verses give us in symbolism steps in the formation of this inner "kingdom". It is indeed true that we must repent and do away with those sins that do easily beset us. If we do not we will not be successful in bringing this regenerative process to proper conclusion.

"And Jesus, walking by the sea of Galilee, saw two brethren, Simon called Peter, and Andrew his brother, casting a net into the sea: for they were fishers. And he saith unto them, Follow me, and I will make you fishers of men. And they straightway left their nets, and followed him."

Simon, called Peter, and Andrew, his brother, represent two faculties within the body. The Christ Within calls to them and they respond, adding two more phases of the being to the work of purification. Each of us must in time call the "Simon" and the "Andrew" within ourselves to assist in the work of "preaching the Gospel" (or enlightening) all the "world" of our being. We do this in living the life of the Christ Within. This finally brings us to illumination, which comes as a result of the "crucifixion" or final freedom of the consciousness from the body. The promise to make Simon and Andrew "fishers of men" means this: A fish represents an unregenerated man "swimming" in the "waters" of the lower emotions. The work of Simon and Andrew in the future would be to raise them above or out of this low emotional life into the bright daylight of the Christian Religion.

"And going on from thence, he saw other two brethren, James, the son of Zebedee, and John his brother, in a ship with Zebedee their father, mending their nets; and he called them. And they immediately left the ship and their father and followed him."

It is possible that the above verses indicate that Christ called these two Disciples from a higher plane. At any rate, their "father" indicates the old way or consciousness. At the call of the Christ they immediately left the old way for the new. And thus, two more faculties of the neophyte become spiritualized.

"And Jesus went about all Galilee, teaching in their synagogues, and preaching the gospel of the kingdom, and healing all manner of sickness and all manner of diseases among the people. And his fame went throughout all Syria: and they brought to him all sick people that were taken with divers diseases and torments and those which were possessed with devils, and those which were lunatick, and those that had the palsy; and he healed them. And there followed him great multitudes of people from Galilee, and from Decapolis, and from Jerusalem, and from Judaea and from beyond Jordan."

The above verses show the continuation of the purification of the body by the Christ Force. The people whom Christ healed represent faculties which become enlivened and spiritualized. The cities spoken of symbolize those regions of the body in which the influence of the Christ Force was active. Decapolis means "ten cities" and this, with the other two places mentioned (Jerusalem and Judaea), reveals the fact that all of the twelve faculties were responding to the Christ influence. The twelve Disciples of Christ also symbolize the twelve faculties, and in a certain sense convey a somewhat similar idea as the twelve cities. A city represents a state of consciousness, as has been mentioned previously, and the Disciples of Christ represent faculties within each of us. When these attributes "follow" or respond to the Christ Within, the twelve conditions of higher consciousness are born.

CHAPTER 5

"And seeing the multitudes, he went up into a mountain: and when he was set, his disciples came unto him: And he opened his mouth, and taught them, saying: Blessed are the poor in spirit: for their's is the kingdom of heaven."

A mountain represents a place of high spiritual consciousness, or Initiation. Max Heindel, on Page 169 of the "Cosmo-Conception," states that when Christ took his Disciples "into the mountain," it really meant a place of Initiation. This indicates that this "sermon on the mount" is understandable in its true meaning only to one who has spiritual perception. That is because it is given on a higher plane than this physical plane and the present words serve only as a vehicle for the concealed spiritual meanings. The reader will have to read with both his heart and his mind.

It is said that a fool in this world may not be a fool in the eyes of God, since the values of this world are not the same as the values of the heaven worlds. The "poor in spirit" represent those who are not haughty and proud of their possesions in the material world, but who go through life humbly and modestly, loving and serving their fellow man. They are not "puffed up" because they realize something of the vast scheme of evolution and their own place in regard to it. Those who have spiritual eyes will never become proud in spirit, because to see things clearly reveals to us the majesty and splendor of higher planes and beings and the realization of how much work there is to do and how far we have to climb.

"Blessed are they that mourn: for they shall be comforted."

It is said that intense desire is the first requisite of an occult student if he is to make progress on the Path. We believe we are correct in saying that soul hunger carried Mr. Heindel to the high spiritual attainments he realized. We are pleased indeed, then, if we have the spiritual development within that mourns or sorrows for a more ideal condition, because then we shall work to better conditions and shall be "blessed" for the work and "comforted" as a result of the work.

"Blessed are the meek, for they shall inherit the earth."

It is not generally realized that the earth is crystallized Spirit. In time it will grow less and less dense until we will again enjoy higher conditions such as the "Garden of Eden" possessed. It is self-evident that proud and selfish people could play no part in such a future ideal condition. This will be reserved for the "meek". This verse also refers to the personal "earth" or body, which when spiritualized shall be ruled by the Christ Within and not the proud and sinful lower self.

"Blessed are they which do hunger and thirst after righteousness: for they shall be filled."

This verse contains somewhat the same meaning as Verse

4. It is when we "mourn" for more spiritual conditions that we are filled with "hunger" and "thirst" for those conditions. In that beautiful book, "The Servant in the House" by Kennedy, the Bishop of Benares tells Mary that she may have anything she wishes. Mary thinks he intends to produce in some supernatural way whatever she asks for. This is not what the Bishop means. He knows that whenever we desire anything strongly enough, we will work for and attain that thing in time. Therefore, Christ is stating an occult truth when he says that if we hunger and thirst for righteousness we shall attain righteousness.

"Blessed are the merciful: for they shall obtain mercy."

Verse 7 very concisely states one of the fundamental occult laws--the Law of Cause and Effect. This is sometimes called the Law of Karma. In the Old Testament it is called the Mosaic Law and stresses "an eye for an eye and a tooth for a tooth." Christ refers to this Law when He states that He came not to do away with the Law but to fulfill the Law. He is speaking of this Law of Cause and Effect or of Karma. Sincere occult students try to balance their Cosmic debts by doing all of the constructive good possible, knowing that even though it does not come directly back to them because of past karma, it does balance this karma and prevents limitation and evil that would otherwise come to them as a result of this same law. This verse could be the subject of much useful meditation, for it is indeed true that "As we give, so shall we receive."

"Blessed are the pure in heart: for they shall see God."

The deeper student of religion fully realizes from his own experience, that different planes of consciousness have different rates of vibration. He knows that it is only that person who vibrates at a high or pure rate of vibration who is enabled to attune himself to the heaven worlds. It is an automatic and unchangeable law that either now or at death we can become conscious of no higher plane than that one to which we are attuned. Since God is Love, Truth, Purity, etc., it is self-evident that we have no consciousness of Him until and only to the degree that we possess the attributes of God.

"Blessed are the peacemakers: for they shall be called the children of God."

Poise and perfect peace within distinguishes the advanced student treading the path of spiritual attainment. Only those who develop peace within are able to radiate that quality. Those who do are surely close to the kingdom of heaven. There is a well-known occult injunction, "Be still and know that I AM God." It is when we still the personality and become peaceful that the "still, small voice" speaks to us and we realize that we are each indeed a child of God.

"Blessed are they which are persecuted for righteousness' sake: for their's is the kingdom of heaven."

When we live in this physical world but are not of the world, there are many "Gethsemanes" through which we must pass. The inharmony and selfishness of materially-minded people will cause us to suffer. The atmosphere of liquor and tobacco will be distasteful to us, as well as many other conditions that go with this world. These things only bring out the beauty of the Spirit in the neophyte, since his goal is the kingdom of God, which shall indeed be his if he faints not.

"Blessed are ye, when men shall revile you, and persecute you, and shall say all manner of evil against you falsely, for my sake. Rejoice and be exceeding glad: for great is your reward in heaven: for so persecuted they the prophets which were before you."

Students of the occult realize that when they step out of the rank and file of the masses, they immediately become the targets of those from whom they have dared to be different. Many times this abuse and criticism is untrue and distorted. Nevertheless, we must learn to take it without resentment and give back love in return, knowing that, "what is mine will come to me," and nothing can keep it away.

In the interpretation given to the Beatitudes we have tried to bring the reader into a certain state of inspired consciousness. We now ask that he re-read these Beatitudes, imagining that the Christ Within is speaking. Imagine the Christ Consciousness speaking to the "Children of Light" or "Children of Israel" or faculties capable of spiritualization within his own being. This is one of the esoteric interpretations of these Beatitudes. It concerns the "attitude" of the constructive qualities within us toward the unspiritualized "people" or faculties. We must continue the work of the spiritualization of the unpurified faculties with love, peace and patience, until we finally convert the whole of the "earth" or body. Therefore, dear reader, do not forget the personal application of these Beatitudes in regard to the conflicting "peoples" within the aura of our own beings.

"Ye are the salt of the earth: but if the salt have lost his savour, wherewith shall it be salted? it is thenceforth good for nothing, but to be cast out, and to be trodden under foot of men."

The spiritual self is the "salt" of the "earth" (body), for without it the body is lifeless clay and is fit for nothing but to be cast underfoot as is the rest of the clay. When we squander this spiritual force or "salt", it loses its apparent savour and the body loses its real value as the instrument of the Spirit. Let us not extinguish the light of the Spirit or lose the "salt" of our "earth".

"Ye are the light of the world. A city that is set on a hill cannot be hid. Neither do men light a candle and put it under a bushel, but on a candlestick; and it giveth light unto all that are in the house. Let your light so shine before men, that they may see your good works, and glorify your Father which is in heaven."

The higher or spiritual self is the "light" of our little "world", the body. All of the "lights" or spiritual persons together are the lights which illumine the outer world. "A city that is set on an hill" means that a state of consciousness that is very high cannot be concealed from others who have spiritual sight. This is because of the light radiation from such a person. This spiritual light or radiation is the sign of the "Master Mason" or Initiate. It cannot be "hid", but shines forth so that all who have spiritual eyes can see it. This is the sign whereby one "Master Mason" may recognize another in darkness as well as in the light. It is not good to repress what light we have because the world needs it. Christ says that if we have the true light it will shine through our good works and we will bring many to a higher understanding, to our everlasting reward.

"Think not that I am come to destroy the law, or the prophets. I am not come to destroy, but to fulfill. For verily I say unto you. Till heaven and earth pass, one jot or one tittle shall in no wise pass from the law, till all be fulfilled. Whosoever, therefore shall break one of these least commandments, and shall teach men so, he shall be called the least in the kingdom of heaven: but whosoever shall do and teach them, the same shall be called great in the kingdom of heaven."

Christ tells us plainly here that although the forgiveness of sins is a fact, there is still the Law of Cause and Effect to be reckoned with. This is the Law of Moses, which still holds good today. It is the law that, "As we sow, so shall we reap." We may be forgiven our sins, but we must still pay our debts resulting from previous destructive activity. Many religious teachers think that with the coming of the Christian Religion and the New Testament, the Old Testament is a thing of the past and something more or less incorrect. This is not the case. We must outgrow, or rather, fulfill every requirement of the Old Testament before we come under the dispensation of the New. It is a great error to teach that all we have to do is to say that we accept the teachings of Christ mentally and all of our debts are immediately cancelled and our sins a thing of the past. Christ distinctly states that He does not do away with the Law of Moses or the Law of Consequence. He plainly states that whoever teaches any untrue doctrine such as the commonly taught one concerning the evasion of our Cosmic debts will surely have to pay for giving out such an untrue teaching. He teaches distinctly that the breaking of any law must be paid for in full, which is good, sound common sense and in accord with true occult teaching.

"For I say unto you, That except your righteousness shall exceed the righteousness of the scribes and Pharisees, ye shall in no case enter into the kingdom of heaven."

The scribes and Pharisees were concerned with the keeping of the letter of the law. We can never enter into the heaven worlds merely with this state of consciousness. It requires intense feeling generated by soul hunger. The mere technical knowledge or keeping of the form side of any religion will never generate this lifting power of the Spirit. Only a pure heart can raise us to the Throne of God. Justification, the Christ tells us, is not enough. It requires CONSECRATION.

"Ye have heard that it was said by them of old time, Thou shalt not kill; and whosoever shall kill shall be in danger of the judgment. But I say unto you, That whosoever is angry with his brother without a cause shall be in danger of the judgment; and whosoever shall say to his brother: Raca, shall be in danger of the council; but whosoever shall say Thou fool, shall be in danger of hell fire."

Anger without cause will bring judgment upon the person when he passes out of physical life and the Ego or Spirit reviews the life just lived in the physical world. This is a process of retrospection or judgment we all go through after death. The "council" is the spiritual hierarchy or its agents who assist us to know and correct our mistakes when we pass out of the body and review the last life. The "fire" or "hell" that we are in danger of when we call our brother a fool is the "fire" of Purgatory. This is not a physical fire. It is the "fire" of the conscience which burns deep into the memory the remorse felt by the Spirit when it reviews or retrospects these evil deeds or words. (A study of the "Rosicrucian Cosmo-Conception" by Max Heindel will explain this process in detail).

"Therefore if thou bring thy gift to the altar, and there rememberest that thy brother hath ought against thee; Leave there thy gift before the altar, and go thy way; first be reconciled to thy brother, and then come and offer thy gift".

Occultism teaches us that it is not so much the gift itself

but the spirit in which the gift is offered that is pleasing to God. The mite of the widow was worth more to God than the large donations of the wealthy men. Esoterically, the above verses teach us a lesson of practicality: that it is better first to be at peace with our fellow man before we enter into our religious rites. We can only perform our religious rites satisfactorily when our hearts are at peace with our fellow man.

"Agree with thine adversary quickly, whilst thou art in the way with him; lest at any time the adversary deliver thee to the judge, and the judge deliver thee to the officer and thou be cast into prison. Verily I say unto thee, Thou shalt by no means come out thence, till thou hast paid the uttermost farthing."

We are taught that if we allow a misunderstanding or sin to grow until it becomes so great that it produces destructive activity, the Lords of Destiny will be forced to see that we are given the corresponding limitation as a result of breaking Cosmic law. We will then be forced to pay the debt which we will have thereby incurred, which will hold us back in our evolutionary process until this particular lesson is learned. In other words, we must try to correct our faults and misunderstandings before they become great enough to cause us trouble of a serious nature. The retrospection exercise given by the Rosicrucian School is very efficient in helping us to carry out this injunction of the Christ.

"Ye have heard that it was said by them of old time, Thou shalt not commit adultery: But I say unto you, That whosoever looketh on a woman to lust after her hath committed adultery with her already in his heart".

We know that "the thought is father to the deed," and in our spiritual development we know well that thoughts are THINGS. We must, therefore, not only master our physical activities, but we must also master our very thoughts. The three steps on the path to spiritual attainment are: First, mastery of the physical body. Second, mastery of the emotional nature. Third, mastery of the mind.

"And if thy right eye offend thee, pluck it out, and cast it from thee: for it is profitable for thee that one of thy members should perish and not that thy whole body should be cast into hell".

We are warned many times to watch carefully the activities of the various physial senses, so that through them or one of them the whole being is not made to suffer. The majority of mankind suffer today because of lack of control over the tongue. Others suffer from lack of control of the lower emotional nature. As we are motivated almost entirely through desire, it is little wonder that our senses lead us astray. Thralldom to the senses is responsible for our limitations. Overcoming this is the great step on the occult path. As Goethe says, "From every power that holds the world in chains, man liberates himself when self-control he gains."

"And if thy right hand offend thee, cut it off, and cast it from thee: for it is profitable for thee that one of thy members should perish, and not that thy whole body should be cast into hell".

The above verse expresses practically the same thought as Verse 29, with one exception. The right hand indicates activity under our own control, since the right hand, esoterically, signifies control. Therefore, the Christ wished particularly to emphasize the seriousness of *deliberately* committing a sin. It is bad enough to sin through weakness or ignorance, but to sin deliberately brings a much greater penalty.

"It hath been said, Whosoever shall put away his wife, let him give her a writing of divorcement: But I say unto you, That whosoever shall put away his wife, saving for the cause of fornication, causeth her to commit adultery: and whosoever shall marry her that is divorced committeth adultery."

There may be several meanings to the above verses. We suggest much mediation on the part of the reader. The first verse probably has to do with the old law. Under this law, and possibly in some Eastern teachings today, a man could leave his wife for several reasons. One reason was so that he might devote his time entirely to spiritual work. It is said that Rasputin left his home and family for that purpose. There is a legend concerning Buddha that is somewhat similar. The teaching of Christ and the Rosicrucian Philosophy give a very different idea. We are taught esoterically, and also as a matter of good common sense, that if we do not successfully carry out one contract, we can hardly be trusted to carry out another. Marriage is a contract and if we fail to do our part in this contract, we are laying the ground work for a failure along some other line. Kindly note that Rasputin's absence from his family was but temporary and that he continued to be married to his wife as long as he lived.

Another suggested meaning to Verses 30 and 31 is this: "wife" means the heart or emotional nature. The mind must not "put away" or overrule the intuitive or emotional self unless it be that the intuition is of a low nature ("fornication"). Whoever takes up with this "wife" or low emotion naturally commits "fornication". This would be the esoteric meaning of these two verses.

"Again, ye have heard that it hath been said by them of old time, Thou shalt not forswear thyself, but shalt perform unto the Lord thine oaths: But I say unto you, Swear not at all; neither by heaven; for it is God's throne: Nor by the earth; for it is His footstool; neither by Jerusalem; for it is the city of the great King. Neither shalt thou swear by the head, because thou canst not make one hair white or black. But let your communication be, Yea, yea; Nay, nay: for whatsoever is more than these cometh of evil."

If the reader will analyze his feelings when taking an oath, he will notice that the emotional power put into the swearing takes him far away from the "peace that passes all understanding". This refers to the ordinary oath of the physical world. The writer believes that this undesirable emotional state was one of the things the Christ wished us to avoid. In the Rosicrucian work no oath is ever taken. Instead, a promise is made, not to any other person, but between the lower and the higher self of one person. The promise is made to your own higher self. The Quakers recognized this and have tried to live these verses literally. Our reputation for keeping our word should be so well known that no bond or oath should ever be required of us. It should not be necessary for us to swear to any promise if our characters are good enough and known to be so. Swearing to perform an obligation at certain times has a tendency to make our ordinary promises worth less. This is one of the reasons that an oath has a tendency to undermine our characters. Meditation on the verses above, with our explanation, should make this part of the Scriptures very clear.

"Ye have heard that it hath been said, An eye for an eye, and a tooth for a tooth: But I say unto you, That ye resist not evil: but whosoever shall smite thee on thy right cheek, turn to him the other also. And if any man will sue thee at the law, and take away thy coat, let him have thy cloak also. And whosoever shall compel thee to go a mile, go with him twain. Give to him that asketh thee, and from him that would borrow of thee, turn not thou away. Ye have heard that it hath been said, Thou shalt love thy neighbour, and hate thine enemy. But I say unto you, Love your enemies, bless them that curse you, do good to them that hate you, and pray for them which despitefully use you and persecute you; That ye may be the children of your Father which is in heaven: for he maketh his sun to rise on the evil and on the good, and sendeth rain on the just and on the unjust. For if ye love them which love you, what reward have ye? do not even the publicans the same? And if ye salute your brethren only, what do ye more than others? do not even the publicans so? Be ye therefore perfect, even as your Father which is in heaven is perfect."

The esoteric principle revealed in the preceding verses is that it is not of the most importance what happens to us, but what is vitally important is OUR REACTION. It does not matter that the man knocks out our teeth or strikes us on the cheek. That has not hurt our character nor lessened our chances of entering the kingdom of heaven. If a man sues us at law or compels us to walk a mile, that has not hurt us. But if we knock the other man's teeth out in retaliation or strike him in return when he smites our cheek, we have injured ourselves terribly. It is unimportant that we may have won a physical battle or a law suit. It is vitally important that we have assumed a pugnacious, or revengeful or vindictive attitude. Such an attitude reveals a character that can never enter into the higher consciousness.

Neither must we be envious when we see others prosper who do not live the higher life. It is not important that the man prosper or not. It is our REACTION toward his prosperity that is vitally important. It is the feeling of the Spirit Within that is worth while. What we gain in this world or lose is unenduring. The treasure which we store up, both in our characters and in the Cosmic Bank, through loving, self-forgetting service, is the only treasure that endures. When we send out thoughts of love to those who persecute us, that love helps to make them kinder toward us, and at the same time raises ourselves to a more sublime state of consciousness. When we send out angry or evil thoughts, on the other hand, it tears US down in addition to hurting those to whom we send these thoughts. That is, providing, of course, that the recipient has anything of a like nature in his make-up to which our ugly thoughts are attuned or may attach themselves.

Christ says that only GOOD pays, regardless of how we are treated by others or what seems to be profitable from the physical viewpoint.

CHAPTER 6

"Take heed that ye do not your alms before men, to be seen of them: otherwise ye have no reward of your Father which is in heaven. Therefore when thou doest thine alms, do not sound a trumpet before thee, as the hypocrites do in the synagogues and in the streets, that they may have glory of men. Verily I say unto you, They have their reward. But when thou doest alms, let not thy left hand know what thy right hand doeth: That thine alms may be in secret: and thy Father which seeth in secret himself shall reward thee openly."

The instructions contained in the Sixth Chapter of Matthew are among the most important in the whole of the Bible, providing they are understood in their esoteric meaning. The interesting and popular novel, "'Magnificent Obsession" by Lloyd Douglas is written around this Chapter. We suggest that "Magnificent Obsession", be read at this time in conjunction with this study. We feel sure that the result will be an expansion of consciousness on the part of the reader.

Christ tells us that when we do a good deed, unless we conserve the power or reward which comes to us automatically as Cosmic credit, we shall not have it as an available force which acts as an actual power to carry us on to higher accomplishments. In other words, when we do a good deed we earn a spiritual credit. This credit, at dividend-paying times as revealed by the stars, comes to us as a power with which we may achieve success. That is, provided we do not exhaust or spend this credit immediately through self-appreciation or appreciation by others. The average person loses all or most of his Cosmic credits either by boasting of his good works himself or allowing others to pay him with their praises. The doer of a good deed in that way loses much of the real value of his work. When the credit for a good deed is thus used up or taken physically, there will be no Cosmic credit with the Father for use in the future. Therefore, we are warned not to talk (or allow anyone else to talk) concerning any good we may do. For this reason, whenever the Christ did a kind deed, he warned the person or persons whom he benefited to "see that ye tell no man". He repeated this injunction many times. The purpose of the many repetitions was to try to impress upon the deeper student the value of this occult law.

"And when thou prayest, thou shalt not be as the hypocrites are: for they love to pray standing in the synagogues and in the corners of the streets, that they may be seen of men. Verily I say unto you, They have their reward. But thou, when thou prayest, enter into thy closet, and when thou hast shut thy door, pray to thy Father which is in secret; and thy Father which seeth in secret shall reward thee openly. But when ye pray, use not vain repetitions, as the heathen do: for they think that they shall be heard for their much speaking. Be not ye therefore like unto them: for your Father knoweth what things ye have need of, before ye ask him."

Again Christ tells us not to spend any Cosmic merit or credit that we may acquire, through physical reward or recognition. This applies to prayer as well as to good deeds. If we wish our prayers answered we must not spend the force of them through being heard by our fellow man and in obtaining merit for our piety. We must speak only to God. We are clearly shown that it is the spirit of the prayer and not the form or its length that counts. We are also warned not to beg our Father for things to satisfy our personal desires. He knows already what we need before we ask Him. We only know what we want. He knows what we really need. Our prayers should actually be in the form of praise and adoration. Many among even occult students do not know the real meaning and object of prayer or how to pray. No petition to God that is selfish can possibly be called a prayer. This is the first thing we must burn with glowing letters into our consciousness. As to method of prayer, we are told to "enter into our closet". This phrase conceals an esoteric principle. That is, we should have a certain "closet" or sacred place where we pray. This place should be used for no other purpose. In this way we build a little spiritual temple which exalts and raises us closer to God every time we enter it. Those who have spiritual eyes can even see its formation. Since prayer is a means of powerful concentration, it is best never to allow any thought to enter into the prayer which is not so high and beautiful. Otherwise, we might ignorantly harm ourselves by concentrating strongly upon the acquisition of some material object. The latter is not prayer. The complete and all-inclusive prayer is the "Lord's Prayer", which follows:

'After this manner therefore pray ye: Our Father which art in heaven, Hallowed be thy name. Thy kingdom come. Thy will be done in earth, as it is in heaven. Give us this day our daily bread. And forgive us our debts, as we forgive our debtors. And lead us not into temptation but deliver us from evil: For thine is the kingdom, and the power, and the glory for ever. Amen."

This is the perfect prayer. It scientifically feeds and builds every phase of our being, both spiritual and physical. An explanation in detail of the esoteric interpretation of the "Lord's Prayer," would be a small book in itself. We therefore refer the reader to the Rosicrucian Cosmo-Conception, Pages 462 to 466. If the reader does not have this book, send to the Rosicrucian Fellowship of Oceanside, California. It is printed both in an inexpensive paper edition and in the regular cloth binding We would advise a careful study of the colored diagram of the "Lord's Prayer", opposite Page 464. Do not become discouraged if you are not able to immediately understand what is said concerning the "Lord's Prayer" in the "Cosmo". Anything worth learning is worth hard study.

"For if ye forgive men their trespasses, your heavenly Father will also forgive you: But if ye forgive not men their trespasses, neither will your Father forgive your trespasses."

Here is stated another occult law. It is the Law of Cause and Effect or the Law of Consequence. "As we sow, so shall we reap." We must radiate love and forgiveness, if we wish to receive love and forgiveness in return. The reader must not forget, however, that forgiveness of our sins does not pay the debt. This is another activity of the Law of Cause and Effect. When we have the state of consciousness that allows us to forgive others and then ask forgiveness, we will willingly repay the equivalent of our sin or Cosmic debt to society through unselfish service.

"Moreover when ye fast, be not as the hypocrites, of a sad countenance: for they disfigure their faces, that they may appear unto men to fast. Verily I say unto you, They have their reward. But thou, when thou fastest, anoint thine head, and wash thy face; That thou appear not unto men to fast, but unto thy Father which is in secret: and thy Father, which seeth in secret, shall reward thee openly."

In not allowing others to know when we fast for spiritual purposes, we are again warned against taking physical credit for spiritual sacrifices or deeds that we do, thereby losing our Cosmic credit or spiritual reward. This reward becomes available at times as a definite power. Those who have accumulated it have felt it in the ability to accomplish that which they could never do before. It is a workable law.

At this point, the writer would like to say a few words regarding fasting. It is his opinion that the ancient spiritual custom of fasting is entirely too much neglected by the searcher-after-truth today. He knows, however, that if a fast is carried on without sufficient knowledge and experience concerning its effects, that it can do much physical harm. When properly conducted, it is one of the greatest helps to enlightenment. It is called to the neophyte's attention not once but many times in the Bible.

"Lay not up for yourselves treasures upon earth, where moth and rust doth corrupt, and where thieves break through and steal: But lay up for yourselves treasures in heaven, where neither moth nor rust doth corrupt, and where thieves do not break through nor steal. For where your treasure is, there will your heart be also."

We realize that we cannot serve two masters well. Life is a struggle between the physical and the spiritual. We know that the higher and the lower within are always opposed to each other. We must in time come into the realization that we are but stewards of anything of physical substance that we may have or use. Even the atoms of our bodies at death are restored to their original form, and are afterwards re-assembled to form the bodies of other Egos. We are admonished to center our minds and hearts on the spiritual things which will endure and not on physical things, which are but transient. As a suggestion in maintaining a spiritual attitude and holding the mind on worth while things, try to imagine that each day is the last day you have to live on earth. Go through each day exactly as if this were true. You will find it a good spiritual exercise.

"The light of the body is the eye: if therefore thine eye be single, thy whole body shall be full of light. But if thine eye be evil, thy whole body shall be full of darkness: If therefore the light that is in thee be darkness, how great is that darkness!"

Esoterically, when the optic thalamus (or the third eye) is lighted with the raised Life Force, it lights the entire body. This is the "eye" that is "single", and as the Twenty-second Verse says, when it is lighted, the entire body is full of light. When we have opened this "eye" we then bear the sign of the "Master Mason". One having this light can always recognize another "Master Mason" who has it, since the opening of this "eye" brings with it clairvoyant sight. When the same force is turned downward for the use of the lower nature, the whole being is in utter darkness, and "how great is that darkness!"

"No man can serve two masters: for either he will hate the one, and love the other; or else he will hold to the one, and despise the other. Ye cannot serve God and mammon."

Mammon usually symbolizes materiality, but it has a still deeper meaning. "M" in this word represents the feminine force. "A" represents the masculine force. Whichever one of these two letters comes first in a word dominates or rules the letter following it. For example, Christ says "Before Abraham was I AM." This means that "I" or the Ego was in existence before Abraham. It also means that before Abraham, the masculine "A" dominated or worked upon the feminine "M" to produce light. This was the proper use or union of these two poles of Nature. When, however, the proper order of things is reversed and the mind or masculine pole serves the "M" (the feminine or emotional nature) then we have Mammonas. This we believe to be the word from which Mammon is taken. Mammon, therefore, indicates the case in which the feminine or emotional nature rules the mind. It is self-evident that when the mind is dictated to and ruled by the emotions, we certainly cannot serve God, particularly if it is the lower emotions. Therefore, the above verse tells us that we cannot allow our lower emotions to have their way with us and serve God at the same time.

"Therefore, I say unto you, Take no thought for your life, what ye shall eat, or what ye shall drink; nor yet for your body, what ye shall put on. Is not the life more than meat, and the body than raiment? Behold the fowls of the air: for they sow not, neither do they reap; nor gather into barns; yet our heavenly Father feedeth them. Are ye not much better than they? Which of you by taking thought can add one cubit unto his stature? And why take ye thought for raiment? Consider the lilies of the field, how they grow; they toil not, neither do they spin: And yet I say unto you, That even Solomon in all his glory was not arrayed like one of these. Wherefore, if God so clothe the grass of the field, which today is, and tomorrow is cast into the oven, shall he not much more clothe you, O ye of little faith? Therefore take no thought, saying, What shall we eat? or, What shall we drink? or, Wherewithal shall we be clothed? (For after all these things do the Gentiles seek:) for your heavenly Father knoweth that ye have need of all these things."

Christ gives us a lesson, in one interpretation, concerning the importance of the spiritual body or "soma psuchicon", as spoken of by St. Paul. He intimates quite plainly that the spiritual vehicle will be a very glorious thing compared to the physical body; that it will last when the dense body has decayed. He gives a hint (as taught in the "Cosmo-Conception") that this etheric body (as symbolized by the beautiful lilies of the field) will be our next vehicle and the one we should work on to bring it to practical use. The "fowls of the air" represent thoughts. The Father feeding them indicates that we will be given wisdom from the Father in the heaven worlds. Next, it is indicated that, like the lilies in the field, we will be "clothed" with this new and heavenly raiment, which will be everlasting in comparison to the physical body. He says that the Gentiles seek after physical things. Do not have the wrong conception of the meaning of the word, Gentile. A "Gentile" is one who is not circumcised, in Bible symbolism. "Circumcision" means the giving up of the lower (symbolized by foreskin) for the sake of an ideal or God. Therefore, circumcision symbolically represents consecration to a higher life. A man may be racially of any strain and may not have been physically circumcised and still be a "Jew" or consecrated one in the spiritual or Biblical sense. As the "Gentiles" symbolize those people who have not sacrificed the lower nature to God, they would naturally seek after the things of the senses and of the physical body. Please always remember that a "Gentile" is never referred to in the Bible as a particular people, but always as a type of individual. A "Jew" or an "Israelite" is one who masters the lower nature and seeks the things of God. A "Philistine" or an "Amalekite", etc. is used in the same sense as "Gentile" and signifies a person who lives the life of the physical senses.

"But seek ye first the kingdom of God, and his righteousness; and all these things shall be added unto you."

The "kingdom of God" lies within. If we seek this and acquire the power that comes as a result of seeking and finding it, we will be able to obtain anything we wish. We will be able to command the Nature Spirits and make gold. We will be able to change the affinity of physical atoms so that we can not only change one substance to another but multiply a small quantity of anything to a very large quantity, as Christ multiplied the loaves and fishes. When we arrive at this stage of development, however, we will never use this power in any personal or selfish way but only to help others. We will be beyond the caring for petty physical objects which so influence our lives at present. We will have accumulated so much Cosmic credit that more than everything we need will flow to us without our asking, just as the verse above says.

"Take therefore no thought for the morrow: for the morrow shall take thought for the things of itself. Sufficient unto the day is the evil thereof."

The Law of Cause and Effect will take care of tomorrow, either for good or bad. NOW is the time we should be careful about, for the present makes the future. If we do well today and the preceding days, we will have a good tomorrow as the result of causes put into action which bring future results. Elbert Hubbard must have realized this Law when he wrote "Live each day as best you can and be kind", knowing that such an attitude would make a better tomorrow. We must have faith in our Heavenly Father and do all the good we can in the little time we have to do it, leaving the rewards of tomorrow to Him. He will surely not disappoint us, since the great Cosmic Laws are never broken.

CHAPTER 7

"Judge not, that ye be not judged. For with what judgment ye judge, ye shall be judged: and with what measure ye mete it shall be measured to you again."

Again, through repetition, Christ impresses upon us the importance of the Mosaic Law of Cause and Effect. He states emphatically that He did not come to do away with this Law but to fulfill it. His chief concern, however, was to fulfill it in the positive, spiritual way through helping us to do good deeds and think beautiful thoughts, which would come back to us in higher spiritual consciousness.

"And why beholdest thou the mote that is in thy brother's eye, but considereth not the beam that is in thine own eye? Or how wilt thou say to thy brother, Let me pull out the mote out of thine eye; and, behold, a beam is in thine own eye? Thou hypocrite, first cast out the beam out of thine own eye; and then shalt thou see clearly to cast out the mote out of thy brother's eye."

The "Cosmo" says, "Looking for the good in others will in time transmute the evil into good." A story is told of the Disciples being nauseated by the carcass of a dying dog. They looked for and saw only ugliness. Christ, however, compared the teeth to pearls. He was determined to be constructive and see good, realizing the effect of a destructive thought upon both Himself and the universe. This does not mean that we should blind our eyes to actual facts, but that we should try to take the constructive viewpoint. All Astrologers, especially, should meditate carefully on the above verses. It is a well-known fact that everything we see is colored by our own emotions and prejudices. If we have Saturn strong in our charts, we see everything and everybody through glasses darkened by this planet. If we are Jupiterian, our "glasses" are rose-colored with benevolence and optimism. Here we might paint a picture for the person whose chart we read so glowing that he would be disappointed because of our kindly exaggeration. We must learn to be impersonal and exact, even with ourselves. Christ says when we see so many faults in our brother, it is a sure sign there must be something wrong with us. We may know that when we reach the point that we see good in all things and all people, that we ourselves are full of goodness and love of God.

"Give not that which is holy unto the dogs, neither cast ye your pearls before swine, lest they trample them under their feet, and turn again and rend you."

The neophyte is warned not to give out teachings which are too deep for the listener. The listener will not understand and will only become antagonistic and critical. In ancient times a man who gave out teachings too deep for the masses was in danger of his life. Jesus Christ, Himself, suffered martyrdom at the hands of the ignorant masses and the jealous priests, for whom His teachings were too highly advanced. Omar Khayyam, in his "Rubaiyat", bemoans the fact that he cannot keep from giving out the wonderful truths which he knows, although he realizes that it will ruin his reputation with the misunderstanding public. The reader will do well to heed these words of the Master and give out only what the listener is able to assimilate, in order not to arouse resentment and to accomplish good.

"Ask, and it shall be given you; seek, and ye shall find; knock, and it shall be opened unto you: For every one that asketh receiveth; and he that seeketh findeth; and to him that knocketh it shall be opened."

We must ask God (within as well as without) for the spiritual things that we need. The verse does not refer to physical needs, since these things come to us naturally as a result of the Law of Cause and Effect when we earn them. Christ asks us to "seek" and promises that we shall "find". This is a most valuable thought for meditation. First must come the strong desire. Then, following this desire or wish, must come activity necessary to produce the fulfillment of the desire. This is what is meant by SEEKING. Only when we truly seek in this way, with the Spirit Within as our guide, will we find. When we sincerely ask for increased spirituality and seek to draw ourselves nearer to God, we bring down the divine power which helps to burn away the "veil" that separates us from the heaven worlds. Esoterically, when we "knock" with the raised Life Force at the "door" of the "third eye", the Ego will "open the door" and the light from this "opened door" will flood our whole being with light. We will then "walk in the light as He is in the light and will have fellowship one with another."

"Or what man is there of you, whom if his son ask bread, will he give him a stone? Or if he ask a fish, will he give him a serpent. If ye then, being evil, know how to give good gifts unto your children, how much more shall your Father which is in heaven give good things to them that ask him?"

Asking for "bread" esoterically means asking for an opportunity to labor in the Vineyard of the Master, since bread symbolizes the result of toil of a spiritual nature. It is true that the Father always has work for us to do when we ask for the privilege of doing it. A "stone" symbolizes crystallization, which is the opposite of "bread". When we ask for a "fish", we are asking for the divine impulse which is born each twenty-eight days, we are told, to both man and woman. We know that the Father will not refuse to give us this impulse each lunar month. Unfortunately, most of mankind play the role of "Herod" and destroy this "child" or impulse when it is born. Its destruction is brought about through anger, passion or any of the lower emotions. The opposite of the "fish" is the "serpent". We are given a hint here not to turn the gift of the Life Force to the lower use, as indicated by the "serpent" of sex. We receive many good gifts from the Father and then turn them into unworthy usage. We are told that God has many gifts to be given to us when we are able and worthy to receive them.

"Therefore all things whatsoever ye would that men should do to you, do ye even so to them: for this is the law and the prophets."

This Golden Rule is simply another way of expressing the Law of Cause and Effect. If we would have friends, we must be a friend first. If we would have love, we must vibrate love. For every cause there is an appropriate result. We must make our causes or activities beautiful and constructive in order that the results which will come back to us will likewise be beautiful.

"Enter ye in at the strait gate: for wide is the gate, and broad is the way, that leadeth to destruction, and many there be which go in thereat: Because strait is the gate, and narrow is the way, which leadeth unto life, and few there be that find it".

The "strait gate" is the spinal cord with its small entrance and narrow "road" or way through which the Life Force must be raised to illumine the being. The "broad way" of the misuse of the Life Force is the way of the unregenerate man and of the masses of humanity. It is only the few who sincerely seek God who find the "way" of regeneration. It is interesting to note that the most travelled street in any city is usually called their "Broadway".

"Beware of false prophets, which come to you in sheep's clothing, but inwardly they are ravening wolves. Ye shall know them by their fruits. Do men gather grapes of thorns, or figs of thistles? Even so every good tree bringeth forth good fruit; but a corrupt tree bringeth forth evil fruit."

Sheep's clothing represents innocence, as the lamb is the symbol of Purity. We are warned not to accept any teacher because of his assumed innocence, but to examine and study his life or the fruits of his work. If the "fruits" or the results of his work are good, then we can know the teacher is good. The life lived and the work done show better than words whether the teacher and his teachings are worth while or not.

"A good tree can not bring forth evil fruit, neither can a corrupt tree bring forth good fruit. Every tree that bringeth not forth good fruit is hewn down, and cast into the fire. Wherefore by their fruits ye shall know them."

Christ warns us that if the results of our lives are not good we shall burn in the fire of our conscience in Purgatory. He tells us to do good works instead of merely making professions of goodness. We shall be judged by the God Within for the actual deeds we have done and not simply by our claims, when the life is ended.

"Not every one that saith unto me, Lord, Lord, shall enter into the kingdom of heaven; but he that doeth the will of my Father which is in heaven."

The "kingdom of heaven" is a state of consciousness and we cannot raise ourselves to that state of consciousness merely by words. This can only be accomplished through doing the will of the spiritual self. For a scientific explanation of how the Spirit works in the body, read the "Cosmo-Conception."

"Many will say to me in that day, Lord, Lord, have we not prophesied in thy name? and in thy name have cast out devils? and in thy name done many wonderful works? And then will I profess unto them, I never knew you: depart from me, ye that work iniquity. Therefore whosoever heareth these sayings of mine, and doeth them, I will liken him unto a wise man, which built his house upon a rock. And the rain descended, and the floods came, and the winds blew, and beat upon that house; and it fell not: for it was founded upon a rock. And every one that heareth these sayings of mine, and doeth them not, shall be likened unto a foolish man, which built his house upon the sand: And the rains descended, and the floods came, and the winds blew, and beat upon that house; and it fell: and great was the fall of it. And it came to pass, when Jesus had ended these sayings, the people were astonished at his doctrine: For he taught them as one having authority, and not as the scribes."

We have a very great and illuminating sermon in the above verses. We are told that when the "Judgment" comes, many will profess to have prophesied, cast out devils and done many great works in His name, but Christ will not acknowledge them. In that day, which will not be the same for any two of us, the mere protestation or claim will avail nothing. Christ, then, in the symbolic stories of the two men building houses on different foundations, shows us how we may secure proper recognition with God on the "Judgment Day", so He will both know and acknowledge us.

Now comes the story of the two men, one of whom builds his house upon a rock, and the other upon the sand. Christ is speaking of spiritual "houses" and not physical ones. We have in our heads a gland known as the pineal gland. It is of a sand-like consistency in the unregenerated man. In the occult student who raises the Life Force to the head or "Jerusalem", the electrical-like Life Force cements the sand-like particles of this gland into a hard white rock-like body. This is the "rock" or "stone" upon which Christ told Peter that He founded his church. He called Peter "Petros" or "rock" because Peter had regenerated his being. The "white stone" of "Revelation" had become a part of him. This is the Philosopher's Stone in one sense. When the individual founds his spiritual self or "house" upon this "rock" of the regenerated self, the "flood waters" of the lower emotions cannot influence him. His foundation is secure. On the other hand, when the "winds" (lower or evil thoughts) and the "waters" (lower emotions) beat upon the "house" of the man who has not raised the Life Force and formed the "white stone", he will be destroyed. The building of this "white stone" of the pineal gland also insures the "builder" against the "second death". Incidentally, this is the kind of "tecton" or builder that Joseph and Jesus were. They were not carpenters in a literal sense. The one who has formed this Philosopher's Stone will also have the wisdom acquired in its formation. He is a spiritual alchemist who has made the base metals of his body into "gold".

It is only natural that the people who hear Jesus give out such deep teachings should be astonished. Although they cannot understand Him, they are able to sense that there is more to His words than they can understand. Certainly no scribe ever talked as this man, who concealed the path to salvation and the deeper mysteries of Life beneath the simple stories that He told them.

CHAPTER 8

"When he was come down from the mountain, great multitudes followed him."

A mountain is a place of great spiritual consciousness. The masses were, therefore, only able to follow Him after He had descended to their level of consciousness. This might also indicate one of the times when Christ absented Himself from the people in order to make spiritual contacts and do more advanced works.

"And, behold, there came a leper and worshipped him, saying, Lord, if thou wilt, thou canst make me clean. And Jesus put forth his hand, and touched him, saying, I will; be thou clean. And immediately his leprosy was cleansed. And Jesus saith unto him, See thou tell no man; but go thy way, shew thyself to the priest, and offer the gift that Moses commanded, for a testimony unto them."

We do not argue concerning the literalness of any of the Bible stories. We believe that Christ could have accomplished more astonishing things than He did, had His purpose been merely to create an impression. Our only concern is with the spiritual interpretation. We believe that the hidden message brought out by this story is this: Leprosy is a disease which starts as a small growth and gradually becomes greater and greater until the whole body is destroyed. It is the disease of uncleanliness. Therefore, we believe that leprosy symbolizes spiritual uncleanliness which starts in a small way and grows until it finally destroys the entire person. This is why Christ usually advised the person, after He had cured him, to "go and be clean". He was advising him to be spiritually clean.

The fact that He advised the leper to "tell no man" emphasizes the occult law we have spoken of before. If we do a piece of good work and allow the person whom we have helped to give us physical credit by singing our praises, etc., we lose the spiritual or Cosmic power which we would otherwise gain. Christ calls to our attention the fact that we must not allow our good deeds to be known of men, "otherwise we have no reward of our Father which is in heaven."

The man is told to offer "what Moses commanded." This is to emphasize the fact that even though Christ had healed him, he would still have to pay the debt which had resulted in the disease as a punishment. Let us keep these two Cosmic laws in mind. First, that all debts must be paid according to the Mosaic Law of Cause and Effect. Second, that when we spend our Cosmic credits by physical recognition or in being praised, we lose the credit or power that we would otherwise gain spiritually.

"And when Jesus was entered into Capernaum, there came unto him a centurion, beseeching him; And saying, Lord, my servant lieth at home sick of the palsy, grievously tormented. And Jesus saith unto him, I will come and heal him. The centurion answered and said, Lord, I am not worthy that thou shouldest come under my roof: but speak the word only, and my servant shall be healed. For I am a man under authority, having soldiers under me: and I say to this man, Go, and he goeth; and to another, Come, and he cometh; and to my servant, Do this, and he doeth it. When Jesus heard it, he marvelled, and said to them that followed, Verily I say unto you, I have not found so great faith no not in Israel. And I say unto you, That many shall come from the east and west, and shall sit down with Abraham, and Isaac, and Jacob, in the kingdom of heaven. But the children of the kingdom shall be cast out into outer darkness: there shall be weeping and gnashing of teeth. And Jesus said unto the centurion, Go thy way: and as thou hast believed, so be it done unto thee. And his servant was healed in the selfsame hour."

The centurion appears to represent the mind in this story, since it (the mind) is of a masculine nature and commands the faculties or "soldiers" and "servants" under its authority. One of these faculties is "ill" or dormant. In order to heal this faculty, it is not actually necessary that the Christ Force contact it directly. After the mind itself has become spiritualized through contact with the "Christ", it is able to restore this faculty to its former usefulness. The true spiritualized mind is humble, as signified by the centurion stating his unworthiness for the Christ to come under his roof. "Roof" represents the head. In one sense, the true home of the Christ is within the heart rather than in the head. It may be that St. Matthew wished to impress this fact upon us.

Since the centurion may also represent the occult type of individual, Christ is surprised at his faith. He would not expect any person not of the mystic or heart type to have so much faith. The "Chosen People" under Jehovah were of the mystic type, and Christ says that the occult type may outstrip the "children of the kingdom" if they try hard enough and the latter become too lax. In other words, those who claim Abraham as their father will be in "darkness" if they rely simply on being one of the "Chosen People" and do not exert themselves. This is brought out in the statement that, "many shall come fom the east and the west and sit with Abraham and Isaac",etc. The way is open to whosoever will come. It may be the peoples of any or all countries and races. There will be no preference made. However, the original chosen ones, if they do not exert themselves, will not be able to meet the Christ at the "wedding feast" of His second coming. If they have not evolved the "wedding garment" or suitable vehicle, they will be in outer darkness. Those who do so, regardless of race or color or creed, shall sit with the Blessed One and partake of the spiritual feast. The "word" or vibration which the Christ speaks within each of us will restore any faculties that are dormant. (This refers particularly to the pineal gland, which must at some time be aroused from its inactive condition).

"And when Jesus was come into Peter's house, he saw his wife's mother laid, and sick of a fever. And he touched her hand, and the fever left her: and she arose, and ministered unto them".

The wife's mother refers to the former emotional consciousness, since the wife represents the present emotional or heart side. The "fever" indicates emotional unbalance or ill-health, which comes to us in the beginning of our spiritual careers but which is done away with at the touch of the Christ influence. Then this heart or emotional nature "ministers unto" us or assists in bringing the Life Force to the top of the "temple" (the body) to illumine the being. In the story of the "Holy Grail", Kundry at the last utters one word, "Service". This may bring additional light to the reader.

"When the even was come, they brought unto him many that were, possessed with devils: and he cast out the spirits with his word, and healed all that were sick: That it might be fulfilled which was spoken by Esaias the prophet, saying, Himself took our infirmities, and bare our sicknesses".

While it is literally true that Christ did all things as reported in the Bible, please bear in mind the personal message to the student of a more advanced status. It is the Christ Within who, ascending into the "dome" of the "temple" (the body) casts out the "devils' or the undesirable phases of our consciousness, by means of His "word" or vibration. The lower phases of our being cannot dwell in the same "house" with the "word" of God.

"Now when Jesus saw great multitudes about him, he gave commandment to depart unto the other side. And a certain scribe came, and said unto him, Master, I will follow thee whithersoever thou goest. And Jesus saith unto him, The foxes have holes, and the birds of the air have nests, but the Son of man hath not where to lay his head".

The "birds of the air" represent ordinary commonplace thoughts, which easily find their way into the mind. The "fox" symbolizes cunning, and this quality also is a part of the being of the majority of mankind. We all have a place or "hole" for cunning in our makeup. However, the Christ or Love-Wisdom principle is still not received into the hearts and minds of the people, or has no "home" with them.

"And another of his disciples said unto him, Lord, suffer me to go and bury my father. But Jesus said unto him, Follow me; and let the dead bury their dead".

Christ means that those who are "dead" to spiritual things might just as well bury those who are also immune to the spiritual life. A man dead to spirituality, we believe, is just as dead in the sight of Christ as one who is laid in the earth. The things of the Spirit are the things of Life to our higher teachers. A second interpretation is, that those who are "dead" to the things of the lower nature had best leave entirely alone things of that kind and turn their backs completely upon them.

"And when he was entered into a ship, his disciples followed him. And, behold, there arose a great tempest in the sea, insomuch that the ship was covered with the waves: but he was asleep. And his disciples came to him, and awoke him, saying, Lord, save us: we perish. And he saith unto them, Why are ye fearful, O ye of little faith? Then he arose, and rebuked the winds and the sea; and there was a great calm. But the men marvelled, saying, What manner of man is this that even the winds and the sea obey him".

These verses illustrate the truth that when the Christ Consciousness is in the "ship" or body, and the "waves" of the lower emotions and the "winds" of ugly thoughts beat against the "ship", the Christ Consciousness has the power to still these things and restore the serenity of perfect peace to the being.

"And when he was come to the other side into the country of the Gergesenes, there met him two possessed with devils, coming out of the tombs, exceeding fierce, so that no man might pass that way. And, behold, they cried out, saying, What have we to do with thee, Jesus, thou Son of God? art thou come hither to torment us before the time? And there was a good way off from them an herd of many swine feeding. So the devils besought him, saying, If thou cast us out, suffer us to go away into the herd of swine. And he said unto them, Go. And when they were come out, they went into the herd of swine: and, behold, the whole herd of swine ran violently down a steep place into the sea, and perished in the waters. And they that kept them fled, and went their ways into the city, and told every thing, and what was befallen to the possessed of the devils. And, behold, the whole city came out to meet Jesus: and when they saw him, they besought him that he would depart out of their coasts".

In the time of Jesus, because of the evil lives led by many of the people, obsession was a common occurrence. Even the obsession of animal bodies by human Egos was so common that many who possessed clairvoyant sight thought it was a natural process. In this way the doctrine of transmigration was originated.

The interpretation of the Bible story is (on one plane) that when the two natures within each of us, the individuality and the personality (represented by the two men possessed of devils) allow the lower nature or "devil" to rule the being, they must at some time give way or yield to the Christ Spirit. Evil destroys itself, as illustrated when the swine ran down into the sea and were drowned.

Another, and perhaps the best, interpretation is that when we allow the lower nature to possess us, we become more and more bestial or swinish until we are finally destroyed in the waters of the "sea" of the lower emotions. Just as baptism raises us above the waters of the lower emotions, so sin causes us, like Pharaoh and his warriors, to be "drowned" or destroyed in the "waters" of the "Red Sea" or lower emotions.

CHAPTER 9.

"And he entered into a ship, and passed over, and came into his own city. And, behold, they brought to him a man sick of the palsy, lying on a bed: and Jesus seeing their faith said unto the sick of the palsy; Son, be of good cheer; thy sins be forgiven thee. And, behold, certain of the scribes said within themselves, This man blasphemeth. And Jesus knowing their thoughts said, Wherefore think ye evil in your hearts? For whether is easier, to say, Thy sins be forgiven thee; or to say, Arise, and walk? But that ye may know that the Son of man hath power on earth to forgive sins, (then saith he to the sick of the palsy), Arise, take up thy bed, and go unto thine own house. And he arose, and departed to his house. But when the multitudes saw it, they marvelled, and glorified God, which had given such power unto men".

It is through sin or the violation of Cosmic law that we bring sickness upon ourselves. We may not recognize as being sins, the wrong things that we do. That doesn't alter the case. Cosmic law works impersonally, and any violation brings a punishment. Christ refers to the Law of Cause and Effect working because of sin. He says that it is the Christ Force working in us which drives out disease and raises us from sickness and other limitations to both spiritual and physical health. He clearly tells us not to heed the doubting scribes, who represent the mental type person and the doubting mind, with its pessimism and critical attitude. We are told to take the Christ into our hearts, and are assured that He has the power in the "earth" (body) to cleanse us from sin and restore our former "health". The "multitude" or common consciousness glorifies God when it sees the power of Christ in and over the body.

"And as Jesus passed forth from thence, he saw a man, named Matthew, sitting at the receipt of custom: and he saith unto him, Follow me. And he arose, and followed him".

Even the material phase of life and the material faculties within, represented by Matthew, should follow and acknowledge the higher power of the Christ Within.. This verse also means that even in our monetary dealings, the principles of the Christ should be practiced.

"And it came to pass, as Jesus sat at meat in the house,

behold, many publicans and sinners came and sat down with him and his disciples. And when the Pharisees saw it, they said unto his disciples, Why eateth your Master with publicans and sinners? But when Jesus heard that, he said unto them, They that be whole need not a physician, but they that are sick. But go ye and learn what that meaneth, I will have mercy, and not sacrifice; for I am not come to call the righteous, but sinners to repentance".

Where the Christ power and consciousness is needed most within each of us is at the "sick" and afflicted regions of our being, that this Force may cure us and bring back our health and spirituality. The work of the Christ Consciousness is to "sit" with the "publicans" and "sinners" within us. He calls the erring phases of being to "repentance", and in time brings the whole being to God. The hypocritical Pharisees represent the individuals who keep the law to the letter but not in the spirit. They cannot understand the loving nature of the Christ. He tells them that He is not come to call the righteous but the sinners to repentance. However, they do not think they are sinners, since they keep the letter of the law, and therefore they are in "outer darkness" as far as this "Christ" is concerned. They are in great danger of destruction, for they will not freely acknowledge their sins, ask forgiveness, repay the wrong and become spiritualized. This is the reason the Christ says that they have "eyes but see not, and ears but hear not". They could hear and see the written words of the law or the form of it, but the spirit back of the form was entirely unknown to them.

There is an old occult saying, "There is none so blind as him who will not see". There is a valuable lesson for all in this, and the writer prayerfully asks that the "eyes" of both himself and the reader be opened more and more, so that we may all see beyond the letter into the spirit of the teachings of Christ. Then we will "see" those parts of our beings which are "publicans" and "sinners", and acknowledge them, and then the Christ will "dine" with us and assist us to purify ourselves in order to become His disciples and followers.

"Then came to him the disciples of John, saying, why do we and the Pharisees fast oft, but thy disciples fast not? And Jesus said unto them, Can the children of the bridechamber mourn, as long as the bridegroom is with them? but the days will come, when the bridegroom shall be taken from them, and then shall they fast. No man putteth a piece of new cloth unto an old garment, for that which is put in to fill it up taketh from the garment, and the rent is made worse. Neither do men put new wine into old bottles: else the bottles break, and the wine runneth out, and the bottles perish: but they put new wine into new bottles, and both are preserved".

The esoteric meaning of the first two verses is almost always overlooked by the reader. We believe the meaning is that when the Christ or "bridegroom" is not with us, it is necessary to fast in order that He may come to us. When He is with us, it is the time for activity. The essence of the above is that there is a time for everything. The time to really mourn for the Christ Spirit is when we do not have it. When w have it, it is the time to be "fishers of men" and "draw" the unregenerated above the "waters" of generation.

Christ tells us that it is necessary that a new teaching be brought into the world. This is His new teaching of Love, which succeeded the law of form, although it did not do away with it. It is for those who were able to raise themselves to a higher vibration and partake of this new "wine" or teaching. These few had to make of themselves "new" men since the new "wine" could not be put into the old "bottles" or consciousness. This is also the meaning of putting the "new piece of cloth" into the "old garment". The "new" piece of "cloth" is the new teaching of Love and Wisdom which could not have successfully been placed or "sewn" into the "old garment" of the Jehovistic or Mosaic teachings. Christ says that we need new "bottles" of a higher vibration to hold this new "wine" or the power of these advanced teachings. The old bodies and minds are incapable of understanding or "holding" these new teachings. The new "wine" would destroy the old bodies and minds as a result of a wrong application of misunderstood teachings. Consequently, the new teachings would have been lost as far as the people of the old regime were concerned. One must become a "new" man in Christ to receive and understand the new teachings and graduate from the Jehovistic regime into the new regime of Love.

"While he spake these things unto them, behold, there came a certain ruler, and worshipped him, saying, My daughter is even now dead: but come and lay thy hand upon her, and she shall live. And Jesus arose, and followed him, and so did his disciples. And, behold, a woman, which was diseased with an issue of blood twelve years, came behind him, and touched the hem of his garment: For she said within herself, If I may but touch his garment, I shall be whole. But Jesus turned him about, and when he saw her, he said, Daughter, be of good comfort; thy faith hath made thee whole. And the woman was made whole from that hour. And when Jesus came into the ruler's house, and saw the minstrels and the people making a noise, He said unto them, Give place, for the maid is not dead, but sleepeth. And they laughed him to scorn. But when the people were put forth, he went in, and took her by the hand, and the maid arose. And the fame hereof went abroad into all that land".

The reader will perhaps notice that this story is similar in a way, and yet very dissimilar, to that of the centurion and his servant. In the previous story, the Christ brought life to the mind. Here He brings life to the heart or emotional nature, as symbolized by the daughter of the ruler. The Christ influence is necessary to bring life and love to both the heart and the mind, for both of these poles are "dead" without Him. In fact, as illustrated in the case of the woman (emotional nature), who had the issue of blood (Life Force) for twelve years (since puberty) it requires only the touch of the "garment" of the "Christ", or the spiritualized vital body, to cure this "disease" or failing of the emotional nature as a result of the abuse of the creative function.

"And when Jesus departed thence, two blind men followed him, crying and saying, Thou son of David, have mercy on us. And when he was come into the house, the blind men came to him: and Jesus saith unto them, Believe ye that I am able to do this? They said unto him, Yea, Lord. Then touched he their eyes, saying, According to your faith be it unto you. And their eyes were opened; and Jesus straitly charged them, saying, See that no man know it. But they, when they were departed, spread abroad his fame in all that country".

It is noticeable that quite often there are two who follow Christ or who are needful of His ministrations. This may indicate the head and the heart, the positive and negative poles of being. We are all "blind" through both the mind and the heart until we contact the Christ Light, which opens our eyes so that we can both "see" and know. However, as in the case of this story, we only know and realize this after we have the faith to bring the result. It is an occult fact that until we have the proper faith, we often surround ourselves with a "steel" aura of gray, which shuts out the Love-Wisdom of the Christ and prevents our spiritual "eyes" from being opened. It will be well to meditate upon this carefully.

"As they went out, behold, they brought to him a dumb man possessed with a devil. And when the devil was cast out, the dumb spake: and the multitudes marvelled, saying, It was never so seen in Israel. But the Pharisees said, He casteth out devils through the prince of the devils. And Jesus went about all the cities and villages, teaching in their synagogues, and preaching the gospel of the kingdom, and healing every sickness and every disease among the people. But when he saw the multitudes, he was moved with compassion on them, because they fainted, and were scattered abroad, as sheep having no shepherd. Then saith he unto his disciples, The harvest truly is plenteous, but the labourers are few: Pray ye therefore the Lord of the harvest, that he will send forth labourers into his harvest".

Here we are told symbolically that we are "dumb" or that our words are as the attempts of a dumb man to speak, there being no wisdom in what we say, until the Christ Force drives out the lower man or "devil" and opens our minds. This story is similar to the one in which the Christ tells the Disciple to go to the water, throw in a line and he will catch a fish with a gold coin in his mouth. This means that when the Christ raises us from the lower emotional life (signified by water), nearer to His own vibration, we have wisdom (gold) in our mouths and are no longer "dumb", but speak the words of light and life, to the benefit of our fellow man and the glory of God.

In a general sense, everyone sees in the other man what is in himself. The Pharisees, who were full of evil or the "devil", could only see this same evil in the Christ, and could not see or understand His great spirituality, since they did not possess this quality themselves.

The writer would like to remind the reader again of the blind men of the previous story. You will remember that Christ warned them to "tell no man". In addition to the original meaning that when we do good we should not waste the Cosmic credit due us as a result, by spending it in physical credit, there is also another meaning. This second meaning is that the higher teachings should not be broadcast indiscriminately, but should be reserved for those who are capable of receiving them. Rebirth, for example, was to be taught publicly no more, so that evolution should proceed along material lines until more dynamic power had been developed along these lines. There was to be an esoteric and an exoteric teaching at that time. We are just now approaching the Aquarian Age when the esoteric teachings will be generally understood and used. Then we will have a real understanding of, and will practice, real CHRISTIANITY instead of merely observing the form as we do today, and as did the Pharisees in the days of Christ.

As Christ said, "The harvest is plenteous", or that there are many people needing the inner teachings, but the real teachers who will unselfishly and without thought of material reward work with the people to instruct them are very few. Let us pray that more and better teachers may be developed that we may hasten the day of liberation of the Christ and the time when we shall live and practice real Christianity. Then we shall "know the truth" and shall "walk in the light" and have real fellowship with one another.

CHAPTER 10.

"And when he had called unto him his twelve disciples, he gave them power against unclean spirits, to cast them out, and to heal all manner of sickness and all manner of disease".

Esoterically, the Twelve Disciples represent twelve attributes within, or twelve faculties of being. This is also expressed as the twelve signs of the Zodiac, the twelve sons of Jacob, etc. When the Christ Within "calls" these attributes or spiritualizes them, they have power over sickness, etc., as expressed above. These twelve also represent the seven spiritual centers or vortices of the desire body and the five centers of the vital body which are set into activity by the Christ Force, even as the Twelve Disciples were set into activity by the Master.

"Now the names of the twelve apostles are these; The first, Simon, who is called Peter, and Andrew his brother; James the son of Zebedee, and John his brother; Phillip, and Bartholomew; Thomas, and Matthew the publican; James the son of Alphaeus, and Lebbaeus, whose surname was Thaddaeus; Simon the Canaanite, and Judas Iscariot, who also betrayed him".

The qualities represented by the Twelve Disciples are interpreted differently by different Bible writers. One writer gives them as Faith, Hope, Love, Doubt, Growth of Spirit, Strength, Zeal, Custom, Courage, Passion, Intuition and Knowledge. Another author believes the qualities to be, Will, Wisdom, Activity, Contraction, Expansion, Attraction, Repulsion, Crystallization, Construction, Destruction, Increase and Reflection. Peter, James and John always represent, however, Faith, Hope and Love.

"These twelve, Jesus sent forth, and commanded them, saying, Go not into the way of the Gentiles, and into any city of the Samaritans enter ye not: But go rather to the lost sheep of the house of Israel. And as ye go, preach, saying, The kingdom of heaven is at hand. Heal the sick, cleanse the lepers, raise the dead, cast out devils: freely ye have received, freely give. Provide neither gold, nor silver, nor brass in your purses. nor scrip for your journey, neither two coats, neither shoes, nor yet staves: for the workman is worthy of his meat. And into whatsoever city or town ye shall enter, enquire who in it is worthy; and there abide till ye go thence. And when ye come into an house, salute it. And if the house be worthy, let your peace come upon it: but if it be not worthy, let your peace return to you. And whosoever shall not receive you, nor hear your words, when ye depart out of that house or city, shake off the dust of your feet. Verily I say unto you, It shall be more tolerable for the land of Sodom and Gomorrah in the day of Judgment than for that city".

Christ tells the now-spiritualized "Disciples" or attributes within not to go into, or work on, that part of the body or consciousness ruled by the "Gentiles" or the "uncircumcised" phases of being; that the material consciousness is to be let alone at this time. Christ wishes to spiritualize the "lost tribes of Israel" or to bring back the spiritual phases of the being to the light which they enjoyed before we had descended into the "swine pen" of materiality after leaving the Father's home. The "Disciples" are commanded to "raise" the "dead" centers ("churches" of Revelation) and restore them to activity; to "heal" those phases of the being which are "sick"; and to cast out the "devils" of the lower man which have so long hindered us. These "Disciples" within are not to carry anything of pay with them because they will be "fed" by the Christ Force. The gold, silver and brass represent respectively, the force of the Sun, the force of the Moon and the physical force of the body. None of these are to be expended in the lower region of the body ("purse" or "bag"). The house represents the body, the vehicle of the Spirit or the personality. The Disciples are told to salute or greet each person if that person is worthy. From the personal esoteric angle, these faculties are to contact or "salute" each of the different parts of the consciousness which are worthy of this "salute". The Rosicrucian student says, "May the roses bloom upon your cross", which may convey the idea of a spiritual salute. Those who will not receive the Disciples are indeed in bad circumstances, since a rebuff to the Disciples is a rebuff to Him who sent them. This means that they have refused to receive the Christ Love, and it will indeed be hard for anyone or anything of this nature when the "Judgment" comes at death.

"Behold, I send you forth as sheep in the midst of wolves: be ye therefore wise as serpents, and harmless as doves. But beware of men: for they will scourge you in their synagogues; And ye shall be brought before governors and kings for my sake, for a testimony against them and the Gentiles. But when they deliver you up, take no thought how or what ye shall speak: for it shall be given you in that same hour what ye shall speak. For it is not ye that speak, but the Spirit of your Father which speaketh in you. And the brother shall deliver up the brother to death, and the father the child: and the children shall rise up against their parents, and cause them to be put to death. And ye shall be hated of all men for my name's sake: but he that endureth to the end shall be saved".

Most likely the reconciliation of Joseph with his brethren who had sold him into slavery into Egypt, has been passed over by the casual reader of the Bible without any great thought concerning it. Nevertheless, this is the greatest accomplishment which the neophyte can make at a certain stage of his progress. It symbolizes the harmonizing of the various "brothers" or phases of being into one spiritual whole. The "eye" then becomes "single" and the whole being is full of spiritual light.

The above meaning (Joseph sold into slavery by his brothers) is that which is brought out in the Bible verses we have just quoted. Christ says that the lower consciousness will betray the higher; that the "father", the first or older consciousness, shall seek to destroy his "child", the newer or more enlightened consciousness. The spiritual attributes will be brought up before the "councils" and "governors" and in many cases those attributes, being unworthy, will condemn and seek to destroy the spiritual faculties which have sworn allegiance to the Christ within. The Initiate or spiritual person tells these faculties within himself to be as "wise as serpents". This means to be as wise as the raising of the serpentine force will render them. He tells them to be as "harmless as doves". This means to be as pure as this "serpentine" or Life Force can make them, and that this purity is and will be their protection. The Christ Within warns His "Disciples" or inner qualities to beware of "men", for man is of the earth earthy. The lower self always seeks to betray the Spirit, since materiality is opposed to spirituality. This advice is always good, but especially NOW.

"But when they persecute you in this city, flee ye into another: for verily I say unto you, Ye shall not have gone over the cities of Israel, till the Son of man be come".

A "city" represents a state of consciousness and also one of the "centers". A "center" is a location in the body capable of being made spiritually active, which produces a higher consciousness. When the lower nature "persecutes" or tortures us while we are in one state of consciousness, we should "flee" to a higher state. Are my readers familiar with that beautiful sacred song which tells us to "Fly as a bird to the mountain, O ye who are weary of sin". This has the same meaning as the above verse, that is, we should lift our consciousness or mind ("bird") to the "mountain" or a higher level when beseiged by the lower man or by sinful thoughts. It is indeed true that before we may have awakened or "gone over" all of the "cities" or centers, the "Son of man", or Enlightenment, will have come. This means that the Christ Spirit will have descended upon the neophyte and he will "walk in the light".

"The disciple is not above his master, nor the servant above his lord. It is enough for the disciple that he be as his master, and the servant as his lord. If they have called the master of the house Beelzebub, how much more shall they call them of his household? Fear not therefore: for there is nothing covered, that shall not be revealed; and hid, that shall not be known. What I tell you in darkness that speak ye in the light: and what ye hear in the ear, that preach ye upon the housetops. And fear not them which kill the body, but are not able to kill the soul: but rather fear him which is able to destroy both soul and body in hell. Are not two sparrows sold for a farthing? and one of them shall not fall on the ground without your Father. But the very hairs of your head are all numbered. Fear ye not therefore, ye are of more value than many sparrows. Whosoever therefore shall confess me before men, him will I confess also before my Father which is in heaven. But whosoever shall deny me before men, him will I also deny before my Father which is in heaven".

That the disciple should not be above the master and the servant above his lord signifies that we should not exalt any of our faculties above the Spirit, which gives those faculties life. Some people have a tremendous pride of intellect, for example, and count the mind above the spirit, which is not as it should be. It is enough for the mind to be Christ-like. Those who condemn Christ and Christianity will naturally criticize and condemn His followers. Even the "Gentile" faculties will scoff at those faculties which "follow" the Christ within ourselves. A great part of life is a fight between the lower and the higher. As Goethe says, "Two creatures, alas, are housed within my breast, and struggle there for undisputed reign".

Christ tells us that all things will be revealed in time, and the Rosicrucian Philosophy teaches this. In time we will be able to read the very thoughts of another, as our spiritual eyes become opened. Therefore, we must try first to "convert" the unconverted phases of our nature, and then preach the

Gospel to others. Some day the higher teachings which the inner Spirit whispers to us will be common knowledge. We should not fear or give the greatest value to those phases of being which are able to destroy only the body. We should, however, give much heed to those "people" (or phases of being) which are able to affect the soul and cause us much suffering in Purgatory. As an explanation of the above, we might, through imperfect sight, fall over a cliff and die. We might, through imperfect hearing, fail to heed an oncoming motor car and be destroyed beneath its wheels. The Christ tells us not to worry concerning any deficient or defective faculties, or concerning any physical results which might come because of them. What we are to concern ourselves with is, for example, an uncontrolled temper which may cause us to do a murderous deed. This could cause the destruction of both the body and the soul. An ungoverned passional nature could also produce the same result. These undesirable qualities, or those reactions which show what qualities we possess, are the things with which we should be much concerned.

Again we feel that much is given in these verses which cannot be expressed in words. Take, for example, the verse which says that those who confess the Christ before men will the Christ also confess before the Father. We know that this has a physiological application and concerns the acknowledgment and acceptance of the Christ impulse or force which, when properly raised, ascends the spinal cord to the "Father" in the upper part of the "temple". This process of itself reveals and acknowledges the zeal of the person.

The fact that all the hairs of our heads are numbered indicates the accuracy and minuteness of detail of the heavenly "Judgment Book", which is in the seed atom of the heart. Each of us possesses this automatic record which contains every thought and emotion, as well as every act of our lives. Therefore, the neophyte who is able to read between the lines is cautioned to guard his every thought, since he will have to answer for each one. This time of answering will be when each of us passes out of the body at what is called "death" and the higher self retrospects or reviews all of the records in this "Book" one by one, and the suffering which will come to the clear eyes of the Spirit, as it reviews its mistakes and sins committed in the body, will constitute a very real "hell" or purging process.

"Think not that I am come to send peace on earth: I came not to send peace, but a sword. For I am come to set a man at variance against his father, and the daughter against her mother, and the daughter in law against her mother in law.

And a man's foes shall be they of his own household. He that loveth father or mother more than me is not worthy of me: and he that loveth son or daughter more than me is not worthy of me. And he that taketh not his cross, and followeth after me is not worthy of me. He that findeth his life shall lose it: and he that loseth his life for my sake shall find it. He that receiveth you receiveth me, and him that sent me. He that receiveth a prophet in the name of a prophet shall receive a prophet's reward; and he that receiveth a righteous man in the name of a righteous man shall receive a righteous man's reward. And whosoever shall give to drink unto one of these little ones a cup of cold water only in the name of a disciple, verily I say unto you, he shall in no wise lose his reward".

That Christ came not to bring peace but a sword means that He knew that when His teachings were given out, there would be a "war" within the consciousness of the person receiving them before the old thoughts and emotions could be raised high enough to practice this new teaching of Love. This saying also applies literally, and it is only too well-known what enormous quantities of blood have been shed in the name of the Christian Religion.

The man at variance with his father is the new mind fighting or opposing its "father" which represents the old trend of thought and teaching. The daughter opposing her mother is the emotional nature (new) opposing the older emotions. The older emotions are the "mother" of, or gave birth to, the newer or present emotions. "A man's foes shall be those of his own household" signifies that his foes shall be those within or of his own being. (These and many other of these teachings also apply literally, of course.)

Those who love father or mother more than Christ are those who love the mentality or yield to the emotions more than they wish to obtain the Christ altruism, which is not possessive. There has been a great deal of confusion regarding this verse. Many have found it hard to reconcile with the Love Teaching of the Christ the statement that one must hate his father and mother or lessen his affection for them. It is only in the spiritual sense that we can obtain perfect satisfaction from the Bible teachings. On the physical plane, this verse also indicates those who are firmly in the meshes of the family spirit. They must be liberated and learn to recognize all men and women as their "fathers" and "mothers". They must recognize younger men and women as their "brothers" and "sisters", regardless of blood ties or racial strain, before they can have any consciousness of the Christ Religion.

The cross is the body, and he who does not take up his "cross" and follow the Christ is the person who does not *physically* serve, but who only *mentally* accepts the Christ teachings. In other words, he is not physically active in the service of the Master. The man who is not active in service and who does not show his faith by his works is not worthy of the Christ. "He that findeth his life" is he who values the physical life above the spiritual. He must necessarily lose his personal and physical, material way of living, which he cherishes so much, since that is the way of all flesh. He must, therefore, "lose" this life. "He that loseth his life", or who counts the material life less than the spiritual, shall find the spiritual.

"He that receiveth" (that mind or heart which receives) any vibration of the Christ, receives the Christ Himself, since the thoughts or emotions will then be Christ-like. "Whosoever receiveth a prophet or a righteous man, etc." naturally obtains the reward corresponding to what he accepts or believes. This is just another way of saying, "As a man thinketh in his heart, so is he". According to the thoughts we allow to enter into our consciousness is indicated our place on the Path. An Eastern teacher expresses the idea in this way: "The birds (thoughts) may fly in the air (the mental plane), but I do not have to let them build their nests in my hair (or be accepted by my mind)".

Christ ends this chapter by telling us that if we give just a "cup of cold water" to a little one, we shall receive a reward. The "cup of water" is the "Water of Life" esoterically and the Christ teachings literally. The "little one" is a dormant spiritual center within ourselves and also represents a more backward "brother" in the evolutionary school. "Giving him to drink" means to enlighten him with as much of the Christ teaching as he can absorb. It also means to spiritualize a spiritual vortice or dormant faculty. "Cold water" symbolizes the primary or more elementary teachings. We are admonished to give "milk" to the babes in evolution and reserve the "meat" or the stronger "wine", which represents the deeper teachings, for the more highly advanced. However, we are not to be discouraged at the inability of our "pupils" to understand and receive the stronger teachings, for Christ promises that we shall rceive a reward for any teachings we may give out, even if it is only the most primary, to those who are weakest in spiritual development.

CHAPTER 11.

"And it came to pass, when Jesus had made an end of commanding his twelve disciples, he departed thence to teach and to preach in their cities".

This verse describes the process of the spiritual man or Christ Within in gaining control of the twelve attributes and the enlightenment which comes from this control. To preach in their "cities" (states of consciousness) indicates the increased enlightenment which comes to the faculties when the Christ Within takes control of them.

"Now when John had heard in the prison the works of Christ, he sent two of his disciples, And said unto him, Art thou he that should come, or do we look for another?"

As mentioned before, in one sense or interpretation, John represents the mind and Christ, the love nature when it has been spiritualized. Each of us will at some time ask, through the "John" or mental phase of being, when the pure, sweet peace comes into our being from the Christ vibration, if this is indeed the "Christ" which has come to us, or which has been born within us.

"Jesus answered and said unto them, Go and shew John again those things which ye do hear and see: The blind receive their sight, and the lame walk, the lepers are cleansed, and the deaf hear, the dead are raised up, and the poor have the gospel preached to them".

The pure heart tells the mind that those faculties which were spiritually "blind" have had their "eyes" opened as a result of the work of the Christ Force; those who were "lame", or who did not know how to walk the "straight" road, are now able to do so. The "lepers" are those who were unclean spiritually and which have now been purified. The "deaf" to the Christ teachings are able to "hear" them with gladness. The "dead" to the higher things have been brought to the "life" of spirituality. The "poor" are those who are poor or lacking in the things of the Spirit, and they now have the true teachings preached to them, and consequently are "rich". All of these are the true signs of the birth of the Christ Within. The blind, the lame, the lepers, the deaf, the dead and the poor all apply to the conditions of the higher and finer senses before they have been changed from dormancy into activity by the working of the Christ Within.

"And blessed is he, whosoever shall not be offended in me".

Blessed, indeed, is the man who accepts Christ wholeheartedly and who is so attuned to the Christ vibration that it is not an "offence" to him or a vibration which is contrary to his own natural state of consciousness.

"And as they departed, Jesus began to say unto the multitudes concerning John, What went you out into the wilderness to see? A reed shaken with the wind? But what went ye out for to see? A man clothed in soft raiment? behold they that wear soft clothing are in king's houses. But what went ye out for to see? A prophet? yea, I say unto you, and more than a prophet. For this is he, of whom it is written, Behold, I send my messenger before thy face, which shall prepare thy way before thee. Verily I say unto you, Among them that are born of women there hath not risen a greater than John the Baptist: notwithstanding he that is least in the kingdom of heaven is greater than he".

A "wilderness", esoterically, is a place of preparation, since it is devoid of the allurements and unnecessary hindrances which hold us back in "civilization", where we have become slaves to the senses. Christ emphasizes that it requires a strong and rugged mind (John) to live the life of the pioneer in the "wilderness". One reason for this is that we have to create our own "wilderness" while living in civilization. Another way of expressing the same thing is to do as St. Paul said and "cast off" the many weights that hold us back in the spiritual race. Those who pamper themselves—who wear "soft clothing"--will never become prophets or pioneers.

John represents the mind or that mental enlightenment which must first come to us in order to prepare the way for the pure Christ heart, or the emotional purification which must come at some time to the neophyte on the occult path. We might also say that John symbolizes Understanding.

We are told, however, that as great as John is, those in the "kingdom of heaven" are greater. One reason for this is that they are not required to function through dense physical bodies, which clog and blind the person to the things of the Spirit, more or less. "Among those born of women" represents those who, while they may be highly advanced in evolution, have not yet attained to Adeptship. "Adeptship is that state or attainment in which the individual is capable of perpetuating his physical being indefinitely and no longer dies and comes to rebirth again. As the Bible states it, "Him that overcometh will I make a pillar in the temple of my God, and he shall go no more out".

"And from the days of John the Baptist until now the kingdom of heaven suffereth violence, and the violent take it by force. For all the prophets and the law prophesied until John. And if ye will receive it, this is Elias, which was for to come. He that hath ears to hear, let him hear".

In one interpretation, the kingdom of heaven "suffering violence" indicates that some aspirants have refused to be denied and have stormed its "doors". They have raised themselves to spiritual heights through sheer will, strong desire and drastic measures of spiritual purification. They have caused the "doors" of the heaven worlds to be opened unto them. This shows the attitude of many neophytes who wish to take the short cut of Initiation. There is also another meaning to the kingdom of heaven "suffering violence". It symbolizes the unscrupulous man who would, through mechanical or black magical methods, force his entrance into a place where he is not spiritually qualified to enter. There are two "doors" in the body by which the consciousness may enter and leave. There is only one proper "door". Most occult students will understand perfectly concerning these matters.

In telling of the coming of John, Christ's words are very significant and very easy to understand. He says, "And if ye will receive it, this is Elias, which was for to come". There can be no mistaking the exact meaning of these words. This is a definite statement coming from the Master that rebirth is a fact. The prophets had said that Elias was coming back and Christ announced that he *had* come in the person of John the Baptist. This is the doctrine of Reincarnation or Rebirth, which teaches that a man comes back to physical existence again and again in Life's great school until his particular work is done and his lessons learned. Christ says, "If ye will receive it", which means, "If ye are able to understand and accept what I say". He tells them that the character known as John the Baptist was ensouled by the same Ego or Spirit that had ensouled the body of the prophet known as Elias.

Christ also said, "He that hath ears to hear, let him hear". In other words, if your spiritual "ears" are not opened you cannot receive and understand these teachings. They are only for those students or truth seekers who are able to "hear" spiritually and therefore understand.

"But whereunto shall I liken this generation? It is like unto children sitting in the markets and calling unto their fellows, And saying, We have piped unto you, and ye have not danced; we have mourned unto you, and ye have not lamented. For John came neither eating nor drinking, and they say, He hath a devil. The Son of man came eating and drinking, and they say, Behold a man gluttonous, and a winebibber, a friend of Publicans and sinners, But wisdom is justified of her children".

Christ tells the people that they are impossible to touch spiritually. This is because they are not ready to accept the Christ teachings. John (the mind) came to them and they were not ready to accept through mental enlightenment. Christ (the heart) came to them and they were not ready to be touched through love. Wisdom is a combination of the heart and the head, the love principle and the mental phase of being united. Wisdom shall be "justified of her children". This means that the result or product of this union of the head and the heart will show forth in beautiful results or "children" as a consequence of the union.

"Then began he to upbraid the cities wherein most of his mighty works were done, because they repented not: Woe unto thee, Chorazin! woe unto thee, Bethsaida! for if the mighty works, which were done in you, had been done in Tyre and Sidon, they would have repented long ago in sackcloth and ashes. But I say unto you, It shall be more tolerable for Tyre and Sidon at the day of judgment, than for you. And thou, Capernaum, which art exalted unto heaven, shalt be brought down to hell: for if the mighty works, which have been done in thee, had been done in Sodom, it would have remained until this day. But I say unto you, That it shall be more tolerable for the land of Sodom in the day of judgment, than for thee. At that time Jesus answered and said, I thank thee, O Father, Lord of heaven and earl because thou hast hid these things from the wise and prudent, and hast revealed them unto babes. Even so, Father: for so it seemed good in thy sight".

The writer believes that Chorazin might possibly be identified as the cardia or the source of the Kundalini Fire in the body. Bethsaida is clearly identified with the region of the solar plexus, since this name means "house of fish". It is interesting to note that Bethlehem ("house of bread") also appears to refer to the same region of the body. This would make it no coincidence that "fish" and "bread" are given by Christ both to His Diciples and to the multitudes. Bethsaida, then, appears to be that place where the little "fish" or spiritual impulse is supposed to be born each lunar month. This "fish" must be raised above the "waters" or emotions of that lower part of the body. It must be "baptized" in the "fluid" of the spinal cord and then ascend to the "Father" in the "dome of the temple" (the head).

Christ, however, is disappointed that the spiritual work which was done in these regions of the body was not permanent. The more experienced occult student knows only too well that Christ is revealing information concerning a step on the Path which is steep and hard to climb.

Since Tyre and Sidon or Zidon are the most northerly cities contacted by Christ on His various journeys; since these cities are also close to each other; and lastly, since Tyre means "a rock", the reader may easily understand that they represent the pituitary body and the pineal gland. (Tyre, "a rock", is the spiritualized pineal gland). The reference of Christ concerning these two cities seems to have the meaning that once these glands have been flooded with the raised Life Force, they are more likely to remain spiritualized. This is not so with the cardia and solar plexus regions, as represented by Chorazin and Bethsaida.

These deeper teachings are concealed from "the wise and the prudent", or those individuals who are so considered in this material world because of their diligence in material matters. On the other hand, these teachings are revealed to the "babes". The "babes" are those individuals who are not so diligent in material things and are looked upon as fools by worldly people because they lack great material possessions. Spiritually, however, through pure hearts and open minds, they are able to receive and understand mysteries which cannot be expressed in words; mysteries which are a joke to the worldly wise. We are given the hint to become open-minded like a child and in that way be capable of receiving spiritual truths which would otherwise be kept from us because of being wise in our own conceit. Today the universal question is, "How much is a man worth?", meaning how much money has he amassed. The real difference between his physical wealth and his spiritual development (which is the only enduring and worth while thing) may be considerable.

"All things are delivered unto me of my father: and no man knoweth the Son, but the Father; neither knoweth any man the Father, save the Son, and he to whomsoever the Son will reveal him. Come unto me, all ye that labour and are heavy laden, and I will give you rest. Take my yoke upon you, and learn of me; for I am meek and lowly in heart: and ye shall find rest unto your souls. For my yoke is easy, and my burden is light".

The Father, in a physiological or personal sense, as well as in a spiritual sense, "delivers all things unto the Son". As the Bible states, only that which descends from heaven can ascend to heaven. In one sense, we (humanity) are the "manna" which descended from heaven, and we (humanity) are the "Sons" of God who will ascend again to the "Father's" house.

We will now explain in more detail the meaning of the Bible verses we have just quoted. Since the Father represents the source from which Christ sprang, or the first principle of the threefold Spirit, naturally the second principle would come from this first principle. In the Rosicrucian Philosophy the Father principle is called the WILL. The Son is called the WISDOM principle. The Holy Ghost is called the ACTIVITY principle. Therefore, Christ's statement that "all things are delivered unto me of my Father", holds good in an esoteric sense whether Cosmically or personally, since the WILL to create anything must come first. Naturally, the WILL to spiritualize the being must also be aroused first. After this will has been aroused, then the WISDOM principle (which decides as to ways and means, etc) is set into activity. After the ways and means have been decided, then the actual work or ACTIVITY begins.

Only the Father principle within is able to know the Son principle. Also, when the Son principle has been raised to contact with the Father principle, it is the only phase of being in contact with the Father principle, since it is the only part of us capable of being raised to that height.

Verses 28, 29 and 30 are often used as the words for a wonderful sacred solo. If these words are repeated frequently they will build a very beautiful vibration in the consciousness of the person using this hidden formula. These verses promise Initiation definitely to those who will heed the advice contained in them.

CHAPTER 12.

At that time Jesus went on the sabbath day through the corn; and his disciples were an hungered, and began to pluck the ears of corn, and to eat. But when the Pharisees saw it, they said unto him, Behold, thy disciples do that which is not lawful to do upon the sabbath day. But he said unto them, Have ye not read what David did, when he was an hungered, and they that were with him; How he entered into the house of God, and did eat the shewbread, which was not lawful for him to eat, neither for them that were with him, but only for the priests? Or have ye not read in the law, how that on the sabbath days the priests in the temple profane the sabbath, and are blameless? But I say unto you, That in this place is one greater than the temple. But if ye had known what this meaneth, I will have mercy, and not sacrifice, ye would not have condemned the guiltless. For the Son of man is Lord even of the sabbath day".

As the Bible is a spiritual book, in these verses "corn" symbolizes a spiritual and not a physical food. We are taught very plainly that there is no time or place where the spiritually "hungry" may not satisfy that hunger. Christ is trying to show the fallacy of the type of religion practiced by the Pharisees-- the religion of form. Those who practice their religious beliefs only on the Sabbath and are lax during the rest of the week believe themselves blameless simply because they have adhered to the letter of the law.

The Christ Spirit within is "Lord" of all days, times, and places. It is superior to the body, which is its "temple".

The statement about David eating the shewbread intended only for the priests, symbolizes a rising above the old religion of form, in which certain rites and privileges were reserved for the priests. When the Christ came, the way was open to all and there were no more favored classes. Occult students know that we must become our own "priests" in our own "temple", the body.

"And when he was departed thence, he went into their synagogue: And, behold, there was a man which had his hand withered. And they asked him, saying, Is it lawful to heal on the sabbath day? that they might accuse him. And he said unto them, What man shall there be among you, that shall have one sheep, and if it fall into a pit on the sabbath day, will he not lay hold on it, and lift it out? How much then is a man better than a sheep? Wherefore it is lawful to do well on the sabbath day. Then saith he to the man, Stretch forth thine hand. And he stretched it forth; and it was restored whole, like as the other".

In a Cosmic sense, the Sabbath Day or the seventh day of the week was the day when "God rested". The real meaning of this is that God ceases to direct each move of mankind, as they develop an independent will. As Man developed more and more the ability to govern his own vehicles, God withdrew more and more and left him to work out his own destiny. Of course, he had and will always have, the help of God and other spiritual beings. In other words, during the time that "God rested" mankind became responsible and accountable for its own acts and thoughts under the Law of Consequence or the Law of Cause and Effect. The true meaning of the "Sabbath" has become confused in the minds of the masses and has been taught incorrectly.

The Christ brings out the true meaning of the Sabbath and tells us plainly that it is right to do anything that is constructive on the Sabbath, as well as on any day of the week. He says that man is "Lord of the Sabbath" and should do righteousness on all days. Man must not only be master of the Sabbath but be master of himself as well. He must "rule his stars", as the Astrologers say.

"Then the Pharisees went out, and held council against him, how they might destroy him. But when Jesus knew it, he withdrew himself from thence: and great multitudes followed him, and he healed them all; And charged them that they should not make him known: That it might be fulfilled which was spoken by Esaias the prophet, saying, Behold my servant, whom I have chosen; my beloved, in whom my soul is well pleased: I will put my spirit upon him, and he shall shew judgment to the Gentiles. He shall not strive nor cry; neither shall any man hear his voice in the streets. A bruised reed shall he not break, and smoking flax shall he not quench, till he send forth judgment unto victory. And in his name shall the Gentiles trust".

As mentioned previously, the Pharisees represent those who observe merely the letter of the law or the religion of form. This type is always opposed to the Spirit, as represented by the Christ. These qualities within ourselves are always "holding council" as to how they may destroy the Christ Spirit within each of us. Please meditate on this, if you are inclined to hew to the letter of the law and to forget the spirit of the Christ teachings. Even in so mundane a thing as the infantry drill regulations of the United States Army used during the World War a paragraph reads, "Quibbling over the minutiae of detail is indicative of failure to grasp the subject".

Christ's healing of the multitudes refers to the fact that the Christ Within will heal the "multitudes" of inharmonies of all kinds that exist within us, both physically and spiritually, if we will but follow the Christ.

That Christ will "show judgment to the Gentiles" means that the Spirit Within will bring the "uncircumcised" or unpurified phases of the being ("Gentiles") to understanding. However, He will not "strive" with us or force Himself upon us. He will not "cry in the streets". "Street" represents the spinal cord, and the above phrase means that the Christ Force will not force the spinal "fire" along the spinal cord or raise it without our knowledge. We of ourselves, because of the Spirit Within, must voluntarily cultivate this force. Christ will not "break the bruised reed" or the spinal cord which is suffering from the injury caused by the misuse of the Life Force. He will not "quench the smoke of the flax" or diminish the fire of the kundalini, but will convert it to the higher use and bring about a spiritual victory. The "Gentiles" within each of us will then be "converted" and "circumcised" spiritually and will come to trust in this new power.

"Then was brought unto him one possessed with a devil, blind, and dumb: and he healed him, insomuch that the blind and dumb both spake and saw. And all the people were amazed, and said, Is not this the son of David? But when the Pharisees heard it, they said, This fellow doth not cast out devils, but by Beelzebub the prince of the devils. And Jesus knew their thoughts, and said unto them, Every kingdom divided against itself is brought to desolation; and every city or house divided against itself shall not stand: And if Satan cast out Satan, he is divided against himself: how shall then his kingdom stand? And if I by Beelzebub cast out devils, by whom do your children cast them out? therefore they shall be your judges. But if I cast out devils by the Spirit of God, then the kingdom of God is come unto you. Or else how can one enter into a strong man's house, and spoil his goods, except he first bind the strong man? and then he will spoil his house".

The writer believes implicitly in all of the stories of the healings and miracles performed by the Christ as related in the Bible. Esoterically, however, the casting out of the devil and the healing of the blind and the dumb is simply the "casting out" of devilish phases of our being by the Christ Spirit, and the "healing" of various attributes or faculties which have formerly been "dumb" and "blind". When we are healed by the Christ Spirit and begin to preach the higher doctrine, that phase of our minds symbolized by the Pharisees will attempt to hinder the expression of the Christ within us at every opportunity.

The "house divided against itself" well represents the present condition of the majority of humanity. "House" symbolizes the physical body. This "house" is divided against itself because most of us possess two distinct natures, a high and a low which dwell within our "house". Naturally these are antagonistic to each other. In time this divided condition will become our downfall unless the Christ Within drives out the lower man. We will know that this is the Christ Spirit which is "healing" us because the devil would not, as Christ says, drive out the devil.

"He that is not with me is against me; and he that gathereth not with me scattereth abroad. Wherefore I say unto you, All manner of sin and blasphemy shall be forgiven unto men: but the blasphemy against the Holy Ghost shall not be forgiven unto men. And whosoever speaketh a word against the Son of man, it shall be forgiven him: but whosoever speaketh against the Holy Ghost, it shall not be forgiven him, neither in this world, neither in the world to come. Either make the tree good, and his fruit good; or else make the tree corrupt, and his fruit corrupt; for the tree is known by his fruit. O generation of vipers, how can ye, being evil, speak good things? for out of the abundance of the heart the mouth speaketh. A good man out of the good treasure of the heart bringeth forth good things; and an evil man out of the evil treasure bringeth forth evil things. But I say unto you, That every idle word that men shall speak they shall give account thereof in the day of judgment. For by thy words thou shalt be justified, and by thy words thou shalt be condemned".

The beginning of the above verses, "He that is not with me, etc.", means that those who are with the Christ will retain the Life Force to be used in regeneration, but those who are against Him will "scatter abroad" this Force in sensuality, and will not live the pure life which stamps a follower of Christ. This is the meaning of the statement that sins against the Christ shall be forgiven, but sins against the Holy Ghost will not be forgiven, since the Holy Ghost has charge of the creative force. When this force is misused it cannot be "forgiven" simply because the overuse or abuse must be paid for eventually in impaired physical efficiency, both in this world (and life) and in the worlds (lives) to come, until we finally become pure and cease this abuse.

"The tree is known by its fruits", and our bodies and our minds show exactly how we have lived in the past, as they are the "fruits" of our past living. The fact that we must account for every idle word is a hint of the "breath record", in which each moment of our lives, through a scientific process, we breathe into our lungs air that is charged both with the stellar vibrations and the individual vibrations of our own auras. These vibrations are all accurately registered upon a certain atom of our bodies. Every thought and act is recorded. (For detailed information, study the "Cosmo-Conception").

"Then certain of the scribes and of the Pharisees answered, saying, Master, we would see a sign from thee. But he answered and said unto them, An evil and adulterous generation seeketh after a sign; and there shall no sign be given to it, but the sign of the prophet Jonas. For as Jonas was three days and three nights in the whale's belly; so shall the Son of man be three days and three nights in the heart of the earth. The men of Nineveh shall rise in judgment with this generation, and shall condemn it: because they repented at the preaching of Jonas; and behold, a greater than Jonas is here. The queen of the south shall rise up in the judgment with this generation, and shall condemn it: for she came from the uttermost parts of the earth to hear the wisdom of Solomon; and, behold, a greater than Solomon is here".

In the above verses is hidden some of the most interesting and valuable information which we shall touch on in this book. The "sign of Jonas" is the sign of the "Master Mason" and may be seen by anyone with spiritual sight. The masses were not able to see it, but the Master could not conceal it from those who had spiritual eyes and could "see". Peter was able to see it and received the blessing of the Christ in so doing.

The three days in the belly of the whale represent the three days the Initiate of a certain Initiation is said to be out of the body and in a lower strata of the earth This corresponds to the three days following the Crucifixion and liberation before Christ reappeared to His Disciples. This also reveals a great Cosmic truth. We are taught that Christ passed through the nine stratas of the earth into the center or heart of the earth and became the indwelling Spirit of the earth. Christ will remain in the "belly of the whale" or heart of the earth for three and a half great "days" or periods. Previously, the earth had been guided by Jehovah from without. The story of Jonah and the whale was a veiled esoteric prophecy concerning the Christ which was thus accurately fulfilled.

The "men of Nineveh" represent the impure phases of the mind, and the "queen of the south" represents the impure heart side of us; both of which will "repent" and acknowledge the Christ Wisdom. Christ says of this generation that they are so materialistic and worldly that neither their minds nor their hearts are willing to accept or acknowledge spiritual truths.

"When the unclean spirit is gone out of a man, he walketh through dry places, seeking rest, and findeth none. Then he saith, I will return into my house from whence I came out; and when he is come, he findeth it empty, swept and garnished. Then goeth he, and taketh with himself seven other spirits more wicked than himself, and they enter in and dwell there: and the last state of that man is worse than the first. Even so shall it be also unto this generation."

The evil spirits must have a "watery" or emotional element through which to work, as they affect us mostly through the emotions. Therefore, when the evil spirit leaves the person whom it has been influencing and finds no more emotional people on the lower plane to influence (only "dry" places or people without lower emotions) it wishes to return to the first person. If the person has not improved himself meanwhile and barricaded himself against such a return, he will indeed be providing an "empty, swept and garnished house." This means that his being ("house") is still in condition to allow the unclean spirit to return to it. In other words, the evil spirit finds an easy return and it also brings with it this time other evil spirits which are even worse than itself, and so the end is worse than the beginning. This is a warning to us that when we have eliminated evil from ourselves, we must continue to strengthen the virtues we posssss so that the evil will not be able to return and bring worse with it.

"While he yet talked to the people, behold, his mother and his brethren stood without, desiring to speak with him. Then one said unto him, Behold, thy mother and thy brethren stand without, Desiring to speak with thee. But he answered and said unto him that told him, Who is my mother? and who are my brethren? And he stretched forth his hand toward his disciples, and said, Behold my mother and my brethren! For whosoever shall do the will of my Father which is in heaven, the same is my brother, and sister, and mother."

Christ impresses the fact upon us that it is the spiritual relationships and not the physical that are important. Our union together in one "family" group, serving the same spiritual ideal, and not simply the circumstances which bring us together in this physical world in the same family or to the same parents, matters most. As time goes on, blood relationships will be understood for what they really are, and we will think less of the relationships of the flesh and more of that of the Spirit. We are all one great "family"--brothers and sisters. with God as our "Father." We are even more closely related, as Christ says, as "brothers" and "sisters", if we work closely together in the service of the Father.

CHAPTER 13.

"The same day went Jesus out of the house, and sat by the sea side. And great multitudes were gathered together unto him, so that he went into a ship, and sat; and the whole multitude stood on the shore. And he spake many things unto them in parables, saying, Behold, a sower went forth to sow; And when he sowed, some seeds fell by the way side, and the fowls came and devoured them up: Some fell upon stony places, where they had not much earth: and forthwith they sprung up, because they had no deepness of earth: And when the sun was up, they were scorched: and because they had no root, they withered away. And some fell among thorns: and the thorns sprung up and choked them. But other fell into good ground, and brought forth fruit, some an hundredfold, some sixtyfold, some thirtyfold. Who hath ears to hear, let him hear. And the disciples came, and said unto him, Why speakest thou unto them in parables? He answered and said unto them, Because it is given unto you to know the mysteries of the kingdom of heaven, but to them it is not given. For whosoever hath, to him shall be given, and he shall have more abundance: but whosoever hath not, from him shall be taken away even that he hath. Therefore speak I to them in parables: because they seeing see not; and hearing they hear not, neither do they understand. And in them is fulfilled the prophecy of Esaias, which saith, By hearing ye shall hear, and shall not understand; and seeing ye shall see, and shall not perceive: For this people's heart is waxed gross, and their ears are dull of hearing, and their eyes they have closed; lest at any time they should see with their eyes, and hear with their ears, and should understand with their heart, and should be converted, and I should heal them".

Christ being in a ship (which floats above the water) indicates that He is in control of, or is above, the emotional plane. "Water" represents the emotional plane. The fact that the people remain on the shore (earth) indicates their material consciousness, as the "shore" or "earth" represents materiality. Christ says plainly that, although they see physically, they are "blind" spiritually. They have become so attuned to materiality that the higher, finer senses and feelings are "dead" to the heaven worlds. In verses to follow Christ explains, on one plane of consciousness, the inner meaning of the first fifteen verses of this chapter.

"But blessed are your eyes, for they see: and your ears, for they hear. For verily I say unto you, That many prophets and righteous men have desired to see those things which ye see, and have not seen them; and to hear those things which ye hear, and have not heard them".

The spiritual "eyes" and "ears" of the Disciples were opened and they were able, according to their various capacities, both to see and hear the sights and sounds of the heaven worlds. As Christ says, to those who possess the spark or essence of any quality, more of that is given if application is practiced along that line. Those that have not the light of the Spirit will find life becoming darker and darker. This is on the very sane and logical principle that if you work with, or exercise a muscle, it becomes greater. If you use a certain phase of the mind, it becomes more developed. If you fail to use your spiritual attributes, they wither away.

"Hear ye therefore the parable of the sower. When any one heareth the word of the kingdom, and understandeth it not, then cometh the wicked one, and catcheth away that which was sown in his heart. This is he which received seed by the way side. But he that received the seed into stony places, the same is he that heareth the word, and anon with joy receiveth it; Yet hath he not root in himself, but dureth for a while: for when tribulation or persecution ariseth because of the word, by and by he is offended. He also that received seed among the thorns is he that heareth the word; and the care of this world, and the deceitfulness of riches, choke the word, and he becometh unfruitful. But he that received seed into the good ground is he that heareth the word, and understandeth it; which also beareth fruit, and bringeth forth, some an hundredfold, some sixty, some thirty".

There is little need to explain the above verses, for Christ Himself explains them. It is the writer's belief that He does this in order to illustrate how a second meaning may be concealed beneath a parable or simple story. This is a hint to look for deeper meanings in the other parts of the Bible. Concerning "hundredfold", "sixty", and "thirty", these undoubtedly have hidden meanings, as do almost all numbers in the Bible. The "hundredfold" may indicate those who have attained Adeptship or have joined the masculine "1" to the feminine "O" and thus attained to the alchemical marriage within. "Sixty" has the numerical value of "6" and may refer to those who, through work in the Master's Vineyard, have developed the sixth sense. "Thirty", with a value of "3", may reveal those in whom the Three-fold Spirit or Ego is dynamically active.

"Another parable put he forth unto them, saying, The kingdom of heaven is likened unto a man which sowed good seed in his field: But while men slept, his enemy came and sowed tares among the wheat, and went his way. But when the blade was sprung up, and brought forth fruit, then appeared the tares also. So the servants of the householder came and said unto him, Sir, didst not thou sow good seed in thy field? from whence then hath it tares? He said unto them, An enemy hath done this. The servants said unto him, Wilt thou then that we go and gather them up? But he said, Nay; lest while ye gather up the tares, ye root up also the wheat with them. Let both grow together until the harvest: and in the time of harvest I will say to the reapers, Gather ye together first the tares, and bind them in bundles to burn them: but gather the wheat into my barn."

The meaning of this parable should be very clear to the reader. Wheat represents "good seed" or opportunities for constructive spiritual work, as given us by God. Tares represent the opportunity to perform evil or destructive deeds as given us by the lower man or "devil." If we allow the lower nature (the "enemy") to "plant tares" in our being, after they have grown to maturity as evil deeds they will have to be "burned" or expurgated in Purgatory after we have passed from the physical body to that region at death.

"Another parable put he forth unto them, saying, The kingdom of heaven is like to a grain of mustard seed, which a man took, and sowed in his field. Which indeed is the least of all seeds: but when it is grown, it is the greatest among herbs, and becometh a tree, so that the birds of the air come and lodge in the branches thereof."

The little "seed" or Christ impulse, which is said to be born within us each lunar month in the "manger" of the body, is so microscopic in size that it is well symbolized by the grain of mustard seed. When this Christ impulse is properly "planted" and nourished in the body, it raises a "Tree of Life" that gives illumination to the whole being and guides and directs our every step.

"Another parable spake he unto them: The kingdom of heaven is like unto leaven, which a woman took, and hid in three measures of meal, till the whole was leavened. All these things spake Jesus unto the multitude in parables; and without a parable spake he not unto them: That it might be fulfilled which was spoken by the prophet, saying, I will open my mouth in parables; I will utter things which have been kept secret from the foundation of the world."

Leaven refers to the Christ Force, which, when raised and brought into the sand-like or "meal-like" pineal gland, changes the construction of this gland, and influencing every part of it, brings spiritual sight to the neophyte.

"Then Jesus sent the multitude away, and went into the house: and his disciples came unto him, saying, Declare unto us the parable of the tares of the field. He answered and said unto them. He that soweth the good seed is the Son of Man; The field is the world; the good seed are the children of the kingdom; but the tares are the children of the wicked one; The enemy that sowed them is the devil; the harvest is the end of the world; and the reapers are the angels. As therefore the tares are gathered and burned in the fire; so shall it be in the end of this world. The Son of man shall send forth his angels, and they shall gather out of his kingdom all things that offend, and them which do iniquity; And shall cast them into a furnace of fire: there shall be wailing and gnashing of teeth. Then shall the righteous shine forth as the sun in the kingdom of their Father. Who hath ears to hear, let him hear."

Here the Christ gives the Cosmic or universal interpretation of the above verses. The writer previously gave his interpretation of the personal, inward application. We here again warn the reader that all interpretations given esoterically are only the writer's idea of their meanings. Please only accept them on your own responsibility.

"Again, the kingdom of heaven is like unto treasure hid in a field; the which when a man hath found, he hideth, and for joy thereof goeth and selleth all that he hath, and buyeth that field. Again, the kingdom of heaven is like unto a merchant man, seeking goodly pearls: Who, when he had found one pearl of great price, went and sold all that he had, and bought it. Again, the kingdom of heaven is like unto a net, that was cast into the sea, and gathered of every kind: Which, when it was full, they drew to shore, and sat down, and gathered the good into vessels, but cast the bad away. So shall it be at the end of the world: the angels shall come forth, and sever the wicked from among the just, And shall cast them into the furnace of fire: there shall be wailing and gnashing of teeth. Jesus saith unto them, Have ye understood all these things? They say unto him, Yea, Lord".

The "treasure" is, of course, the Christ Spark which we find in the "field" of our being. When we discover this "Spark" or possibility, we "sell" or get rid of other qualities that would interfere with this new find, in order to possess and develop this new "treasure". It is also the "pearl of great price", and we "sell" or dispose of minor "jewels" or pleasures in order to possess it. It is the "light" which floods the whole being when developed.

The parable of the fish has both a personal and Cosmic application. In the personal application, we know that after we pass to higher planes in the "net" of death, which drags us up out of the life of sensuality or emotions (water), the angels and higher beings will assist us in casting out our bad fish or evil as we gradually progress from plane to plane. Some knowledge of the "Rosicrucian Cosmo-Conception" is necessary to an understanding of the methods through which this is accomplished.

"Then said he unto them, Therefore every scribe which is instructed unto the kingdom of heaven is like unto a man that is an householder, which bringeth forth out of his treasure things new and old. And it came to pass, that when Jesus had finished these parables, he departed thence".

These verses indicate that every scribe or writer who is instructed in the mysteries of Christian unfoldment brings forth from his spiritual perception truths which are "old" or well-known, and also truths which are "new" and which, through meditation and prayer, are just being perceived and understood by the scribe. It is the prayer of this writer that something new in esoteric interpretation, as well as familiar truths, may be brought to light for the reader, in this book and in other of his Bible interpretations.

"And when he was come into his own country, he taught them in their synagogue, insomuch that they were astonished and said, Whence hath this man this wisdom, and these mighty works? Is not this the carpenter's son? is not his mother called Mary? and his brethren, James and Joses, and Simon, and Judas? And his sisters, are they not all with us? Whence then hath this man all these things? And they were offended in him. But Jesus said unto them, A prophet is not without honour, save in his own country, and in his own house. And he did not many mighty works there because of their unbelief".

A closed mind is the most effectual barrier to progress that we know. Those who think they already know a thing or are jealous of those who would teach them are difficult to teach. Many people, even though they have studied little, think they know more concerning the Bible and religion than the teacher who has studied, prayed and meditated on this subject. Especially concerning the Bible does each one think he knows more than anyone else. This makes it extremely difficult to spread the inner, esoteric teachings. Christ brings out this fact very plainly. He also shows how difficult it is to convince those who are not open-minded. It is easier to convince a stranger, than one who is close to us. That is why we must try to make our daily lives speak for themselves. We must make our lives reveal our doctrines, instead of trying to put them into words. Max Heindel says that the conversion by Mohammed of his wife to his religion was perhaps his greatest accomplishment. His wife had an opportunity to see whether Mohammed really lived his religion as well as to teach it. It is almost impossible to help anyone against his will or when he has doubt, suspicion or other destructive thoughts. Therefore, Christ could do but little in His own country and among His own people.

CHAPTER 14.

"At that time Herod the tetrarch heard of the fame of Jesus, And said unto his servants, This is John the Baptist; he is risen from the dead; and therefore mighty works do shew forth themselves in him. For Herod had laid hold of John, and bound him, and put him in prison for Herodias' sake, his brother Phillip's wife. For John said unto him, It is not lawful for thee to have her. And when he would have put him to death, he feared the multitude, because they counted him as a prophet. But when Herod's birthday was kept, the daughter of Herodias danced before them, and pleased Herod. Whereupon he promised with an oath to give her whatsoever she should ask. And she, being before instructed of her mother, said Give me here John Baptist's head in a charger. And the king was sorry: nevertheless for the oath's sake, and them which sat with him at meat, he commanded it to be given her. And he sent, and beheaded John in the prision. And his head was brought in a charger, and given to the damsel: and she brought it to her mother. And his disciples came, and took up the body, and buried it, and went and told Jesus. When Jesus heard of it, he departed thence by ship into a desert place apart: and when the people had heard thereof, they followed him on foot out of the cities".

John, as we have said before, represents the mind, and Herod symbolizes the king of the lower nature, Lust. The mind makes it known to Herod (the lower nature) that it is wrong that he should use the Life Force in sensuality. This is represented by Herod's union with his brother's wife. Philip means "lover of horses" and in this sense signifies one who loves lower things. His wife would accordingly represent the lower emotional nature. The "daughter" of the lower emotions asks for the "death" of John, the mind. It is physiologically true that when we indulge in the lower nature, we rob the brain of the force that builds and maintains it. Lust wedded to the emotional nature causes the atrophy of the mind (it is "put in prison") and finally its "death". This especially applies to the spiritual side of the mind.

"And when Jesus went forth, and saw a great multitude, and was moved with compassion toward them and he healed their sick. And when it was evening, his disciples came to him, saying, This is a desert place, and the time is now past; send the multitude away, that they may go into the villages and buy themselves victuals. But Jesus said unto them, They need not depart; give ye them to eat. And they say unto him, We have here but five loaves, and two fishes. He said, Bring them hither to me. And he commanded the multitude to sit down on the grass, and took the five loaves, and the two fishes, and looking up to heaven, he blessed, and brake, and gave the loaves to his disciples, and the disciples to the multitude. And they did all eat, and were filled: and they took up of the fragments that remained twelve baskets full. And they that had eaten were about five thousand men, beside women and children".

The miracle of the loaves and the fishes represents the Virgo-Pisces dispensation or teaching, which was to be given to the masses as their next spiritual step. The "loaves" represent Virgo and symbolize purity and toil in the Vineyard of the Master. "Fishes" are the Astrological symbol of Pisces, the opposite sign of the Zodiac to Virgo. They symbolize, in one sense, that exalted state which will be acquired by the masses ("fish") when they have been raised above the "waters" of the lower emotions. Thus baptism (spiritual baptism) is promised for those people who employ the teachings of the Gospels (which are written by the Disciples or "fishers of men") which lift them above the "waters" of the lower emotions to a life of regeneration.

The number of loaves (five) and the number of fishes (two) added together give the mystical number of seven. The number of men who were fed, which was five thousand, added to the above "7" gives us the number "12". The "0's" are not counted in this instance. "12" was also the number of the baskets of food which remained when all had eaten. We think the number "12", as used in this connection, symbolizes the following: We are told that the seven centers of the desire body and the five centers of the vital body (the wounds of Christ) must be "fed" or opened by the new teaching (Pisces-Virgo) which was to be given at this time.

"And straightway Jesus constrained his disciples to get into a ship, and to go before him unto the other side, while he sent the multitude away. And when he had sent the multitudes away, he went up into a mountain apart to pray: and when the even was come, he was there alone. But the ship was now in the midst of the sea, tossed with waves: for the wind was contrary. And the fourth watch of the night Jesus went unto them, walking on the sea. And when the disciples saw him walking on the sea, they were troubled, saying It is a spirit; and they cried out for fear. But straightway Jesus spake unto them, saying, Be of good cheer; it is I; be not afraid. And when Peter answered him and said, Lord, if it be thou, bid me come unto thee on the water. And he said, Come. And when Peter was come down out of the ship, he walked on the water, to go to Jesus. But when he saw the wind was boisterous, he was afraid; and beginning to sink, he cried, saying, Lord, save me. And immediately Jesus stretched forth his hand and caught him, and said unto him, O thou of little faith, wherefore didst thou doubt? And when they were come into the ship, the wind ceased. Then they that were come into the ship, came and worshipped him, saying, Of a truth thou art the Son of God. And when they were gone over, they came into the land of Gennesaret. And when the men of that place had knowledge of him, they sent out into all that country round about, and brought unto him all that were diseased: And besought him that they might only touch the hem of his garment: and as many as were touched were made perfectly whole".

The high mountain, as we mentioned before, is a spiritual plane or place of Initiation. It was "evening" when Christ went up into this mountain. This corroborates the Rosicrucian teaching that our consciousness functions in the physical plane during the day and on other planes at night. Another thought is that it is usually in the "evening" or latter part of life that we attain to the "mountain" of Initiation. The Disciples were in the "ship", which symbolizes the desire body in this instance, and being on the "sea" shows that they were in the upper regions of the Desire World, since the ship floats above those "waters" which indicate the lower emotions or lower stratas of the Desire World. Christ appears to the Disciples from a higher plane and they are afraid because of the power and glory of His spiritual vehicles. Peter wishes to come to Him, or to go to the higher region in which He is functioning. He tries, but is not able to maintain the rate of vibration necessary to remain on this plane. His emotional nature or desire body begins to pull him down and he starts sinking into the Desire World. Personally, each one of us is "Peter" endeavoring to "walk" on the sea or to maintain mastery over the emotional nature. We shall all "sink" beneath the "waves" in time, if we do not call upon the Master to give us His "hand" or his help. It is only through His help that we are able to function above the lower nature and attain mastery over it. The "waves" symbolize turbulent emotions, and the strong "winds" are strong thoughts of not too high a nature.

CHAPTER 15.

"Then came to Jesus scribes and Pharisees, which were of Jerusalem, saying, Why do thy disciples transgress the tradition of the elders? for they wash not their hands when they eat bread. But he answered and said unto them, Why do ye also transgress the commandment of God by your tradition? For God commanded, saying, Honour thy father and mother: and, He that curseth father or mother, let him die the death. But ye say, Whosoever shall say to his father or his mother, It is a gift, by whatsoever thou mightest be profited by me; And honour not his father or his mother, he shall be free. Thus have ye made the commandment of God of none effect by your tradition. Ye hypocrites, well did Esaias prophecy of you, saying, This people draweth nigh unto me with their mouth, and honoureth me with their lips; but their heart is far from me. But in vain they do worship me, teaching for doctrines the commandments of men".

It is the spirit and not the form which is important from the spiritual viewpoint. In one sense, the scribes and Pharisees are qualities or faculties of a material phase of the mind. These faculties observe the outward form of religion but not the spirit. They ceremoniously "wash their hands before eating", but let their hearts and emotions remain unclean. The Disciples of Christ, representing faculties of the spiritualized being, are unmindful of the form but are concerned with the spirit. With them a clean heart and a clean mind are more important than clean hands.

The commandment to honour our fathers and our mothers has two meanings. First, we are to be grateful to the father and mother who gave us an opportunity to exeperience existence in the physical world. Second, it symbolizes the "father" and "mother" within each of us, the original mental and emotional consciousness from which springs the newer or higher consciousness. The scribes and the Pharisees wish to avoid any obligation to the old consciousness ("father" and "mother"). They also wish to avoid obligation to the older religious forms which are the "father" and "mother" of the newer forms and which raise us from a primary to a more advanced religious grade. In other words, they wish to avoid paying just Cosmic debts.

Christ showed His obligation to His Disciples by washing their feet. As we ourselves advance, because of our work with others, we must realize that we are under obligation to those we work with.

In still another sense, our "fathers" and our "mothers" are those older or more advanced beings who assist us in evolution. We must not only be grateful to them, but we must repay the obligation at some time, in some way.

"And he called the multitude, and said unto them, Hear, and understand: Not that which goeth into the mouth defileth a man; but that which cometh out of the mouth, this defileth a man. Then came his disciples, and said unto him, Knowest thou that the Pharisees were offended, after they heard this saying? But he answered and said, Every plant, which my heavenly Father hath not planted, shall be rooted up. Let them alone: they be blind leaders of the blind. And if the blind lead the blind, both shall fall into the ditch. Then answered Peter and said unto him, Declare unto us this parable. And Jesus said, Are ye also yet without understanding? Do not ye yet understand, that whatsoever entereth in at the mouth goeth into the belly, and is cast out into the draught? But those things which proceed out of the mouth come forth from the heart; and they defile the man. For out of the heart proceed evil thoughts, murders, adulteries, fornications, thefts, false witness, blasphemies: These are the things which defile a man: but to eat with unwashen hands defileth not a man".

Again the emphasis is placed upon the importance of spiritual things and the unimportance of the things of form or materiality. It is spiritual food which is important. It is spiritual cleansing that is important. There is an old Eastern saying that when searching for a master, we are not to overlook a man merely because his finger nails are not clean.

"Then Jesus went thence, and departed into the coasts of Tyre and Sidon. And, behold, a woman of Canaan came out of the same coasts, and cried unto him, saying, Have mercy on me, O Lord, thou son of David; my daughter is greviously vexed with a devil. But he answered her not a word. And his disciples came and besought him, saying, Send her away; for she crieth after us. But he answered and said,

I am not sent but unto the lost sheep of the house of Israel. Then came she and worshipped him, saying, Lord, help me. But he answered and said, It is not meet to take the children's bread, and to cast it to dogs. And she said, Truth, Lord: yet the dogs eat of the crumbs which fall from their master's table. Then Jesus answered and said unto her, O woman, great is thy faith: be it unto thee even as thou wilt. And her daughter was made whole from that very hour."

This woman of Canaan represents the emotional force when it is used sensually. Canaan is "a low country". This woman has a daughter who is possessed of the devil. This daughter represents the product or result of the wrong use of this emotional force. Christ tells the woman of Canaan that He is sent to restore the "lost sheep". This means the lost purity of the "Children of Israel" or the spiritual faculties of the being.

Christ also tells the woman that it is not proper to take the "children's bread", which represents spiritual food for the higher faculties, and give it to the "dogs" (unrestrained emotions). There is much food for thought in this verse. This is what has caused all the miseries of mankind. The next verse is also full of meaning. The statement that, "the dogs eat of the crumbs which fall from their master's table", means that the higher faculties which should be "masters" of the Life Force, unfortunately "let fall crumbs" or part of this Force, which is hungrily seized upon by the lower emotions. When we cease dropping these "crumbs", we shall have no more "dogs" within us.

Christ purified this emotional nature, this "woman", as He must likewise purify our own hearts and cure our "daughters" or products of the emotional nature, until we raise this nature to a higher plane.

"And Jesus departed from thence, and came nigh unto the sea of Galilee; and went up into a mountain, and sat down there. And great multitudes came unto him, having with them those that were lame, blind, dumb, maimed, and many others, and cast them down at Jesus' feet; and he healed them. Insomuch that the multitude wondered, when they saw the dumb to speak, the maimed to be whole, the lame to walk, and the blind to see: and they glorified the God of Israel. Then Jesus called his disciples unto him, and said, I have compassion on the multitude, because they continue with me now three days, and have nothing to eat: and I will not send them away fasting, lest they faint in the way. And his disciples say unto him, Whence should we have so much bread in the wilderness, as to fill so great a multitude? And Jesus saith unto them, How many loaves have ye? And they said, Seven, and a few little fishes. And he commanded the multitude to sit on the ground. And he took the seven loaves and the fishes, and gave thanks, and brake them, and gave to his disciples, and the disciples to the multitude. And they did all eat, and were filled: and they took up of the broken meat that was left seven baskets full. And they that did eat were four thousand men, beside women and children. And he sent away the multitude and took ship, and came into the coasts of Magdala''.

This is practically a repetition or a similar incident in the life of Christ, with a few exceptions. To repeat the esoteric meaning briefly, it tells us of the great spiritual consciousness possessed by Christ (the fact that He went up into the mountain) ,and indicates that He brought down this power to the lower plane for the benefit of the masses with their lower consciousness. The lame, blind, dumb, maimed, etc. shows the various spiritual deficiencies of those who came to Him for enlightenment. Their eyes and minds are "opened" through His wisdom, and their spiritual misconceptions or "illnesses" are done away with. Of coures, this does not mean that the literal story of the healing and teaching did not take place exactly as described in the Bible.

Again Christ feeds the multitudes with the loaves and the fishes, or emphasizes for the benefit of the advanced student the Virgo-Pisces teaching--the doctrine of purity and regeneration which was to be taught during the coming age. It is to be noticed that after the multitude has partaken of the food, it does not diminish, but just as much remains as there was in the beginning. "Four thousand" men may indicate the four bodies or vehicles of man (physical body, vital body, desire body and mind "body") which were "fed" by this teaching. This "four thousand" (which, according to the numerological delineation, is reduced to the number 4 or 40) may also refer to a period of preparation or a fast. These fasts of forty days were undertaken by many of the spiritual pioneers. We will remember also the forty years in the wilderness. While this was literally true, it also indicated the period of preparation necessary before the "chosen people" could be given the new teaching.

CHAPTER 16.

"The Pharisees also with the Sadducees came, and tempting desired him that he would shew them a sign from heaven. He answered and said unto them, When it is evening, ye say It will be fair weather: for the sky is red. And in the morning, It will be foul weather to day: for the sky is red and lowring. O ye hypocrites, ye can discern the face of the sky; but can ye not discern the signs of the times? A wicked and adulterous generation seeketh after a sign; and there shall no sign be given unto it, but the sign of the prophet Jonas. And he left them, and departed. And when his disciples were come to the other side, they had forgotten to take bread. Then Jesus said unto them, Take heed and beware of the leaven of the Pharisees and of the Sadducees. And they reasoned among themselves, saying, It is because we have taken no bread. Which when Jesus perceived, he said unto them, O ye of little faith, why reason ye among yourselves, because ye have brought no bread? Do ye not yet understand, neither remember the five loaves of the five thousand, and how many baskets ye took up? Neither the seven loaves of the four thousand, and how many baskets ye took up? How is it that ye do not understand that I spake it not to you concerning bread, that ye should beware of the leaven of the Pharisees and of the Sadducees? Then understood they how that he bade them not beware of the leaven of the bread, but of the doctrine of the Pharisees and of the Sadducees".

Christ tells the Sadducees, who are materialists, and the Pharisees, who adhere merely to the form in religion, that they see and understand physically but not at all spiritually. They see the physical signs in the sky but are unable to understand the spiritual signs of the heaven worlds. They ask Christ for a sign of His authority when He radiates, even while they are speaking to Him, from His glorious person the unmistakable sign of His spiritual authority and the sign of the high Initiate. They are to be given no sign except the "sign of the prophet Jonas". Jonas means "dove" and symbolizes the pure Initiate. As the Sadducees and the Pharisees have no spiritual "eyes" with which to perceive the wonderful radiation which emanates from the physical body of Christ, the meaning of the "sign of the prophet Jonas" is lost upon them. The only way a true "Master Mason" may recognize another in the "darkness" as well as in the "light" is through this radiation, which requires spiritual sight to be seen.

The "leaven" of the Pharisees and of the Sadducees represent their pernicious doctrines of form and materialism, which corrupt so many who will not or do not open their hearts to the Love teaching of the Christ.

"When Jesus came into the coasts of Cæsarea Philippi, he asked his disciples, saying, Whom do men say that I the Son of man am? And they said, Some say that thou art John the Baptist: some Elias; and others, Jeremias, or one of the prophets. He saith unto them, But whom say ye that I am? And Simon Peter answered and said, Thou art the Christ, the Son of the living God. And Jesus answered and said unto him, Blessed art thou, Simon Barjona: for flesh and blood hath not revealed it unto thee, but my Father which is in heaven. And I say also unto thee, That thou art Peter and upon this rock I will build my church; and the gates of hell shall not prevail against it. And I will give unto thee the keys of the kingdom of heaven: and whatsoever thou shalt bind on earth shall be bound in heaven: and whatsoever thou shalt loose on earth shall be loosed in heaven. Then charged he his disciples that they should tell no man that he was Jesus the Christ".

Christ questioned His Disciples concerning His identity, to test their spiritual sight and perception. They all realized that He was a great soul, but only Peter possessed the clairvoyant vision which enabled him to recognize the great indwelling Christ Spirit. With this vision, of course, would also come a corresponding state of spiritual consciousness. "Flesh and blood", says the Christ, or a physical means, could not have given Peter his knowledge. This required spiritual sight is gained through regeneration. Peter or "Petros" means "a rock". Peter had built the "white stone" mentioned in Revelation (within his being), which is also the Philosopher's Stone, and is produced by cementing the sand-like particles of the pineal gland into a hard, rock-like condition. This is accomplished through the raising of the Life Force and by directing this Force properly when raised.

The opposite type to Peter is the man who built his house upon the sand, which was destroyed by the storm. This is the story of the person who builds his spiritual "house" or "church" upon the foundation of the unregenerated being. It is always destroyed by the "storm" of the unrestrained emotional nature. The man who builds his "house" upon a "rock" is the "Peter" or "Petros" who has regenerated himself and built the "white stone" of Revelation within. This is the Philosopher's Stone or Diamond Soul. No "storm" of unrestrained emotions will harm such a man.

Christ says that the Temple of God is founded upon the regenerated man or living "stone" which is called "Petros". "Whatsoever thou shalt bind on earth shall be bound in heaven, etc.", means that the person who has mastered or "bound" his lower nature on earth will also be master of the lower nature on other planes. The one who "looses" or lets run free his emotional nature will find that it is also unrestrained in the afterlife. We do not become saints merely by dying, and Christ tells His Disciples that restrained qualities here in the physical world will be restrained after death.

"From that time forth began Jesus to shew his disciples, how that he must go unto Jerusalem, and suffer many things of the elders and chief priests and scribes, and be killed, and be raised again the third day. Then Peter took him, and began to rebuke him, saying, Be it far from thee, Lord: this shall not be unto thee. But he turned, and said unto Peter, Get thee behind me, Satan: thou art an offence unto me: for thou savourest not the things that be of God, but those that be of men. Then said Jesus unto his disciples, If any man will come after me, let him deny himself, and take up his cross, and follow me. For whosoever will save his life shall lose it: and whosoever will lose his life for my sake shall find it. For what is a man profited, if he shall gain the whole world, and lose his own soul? or what shall a man give in exchange for his soul? For the Son of man shall come in the glory of his Father with his angels; and then he shall reward every man according to his works. Verily I say unto you, There be some standing here, which shall not taste of death, till they see the Son of man coming in his kingdom".

It is probable that the teachings which Christ gave to His Disciples concerning His life (which is a symbol of an inner process) were not clearly understood by them until some time after His death. Even Peter did not fully comprehend. "Taking up one's cross" and following the Christ represents unselfish service done in the physical world in the physical body. This leads to spiritual attainment.

Other esoteric truths brought out in the above verses are: that we must lose our lives or "die" to materiality before we can "live" spiritually; that materiality is of no value in comparison with the value of the soul. We are taught that spirituality is of an exact opposite nature to physical things, and therefore cannot be discerned physically.

Christ says that He will come again in glory (which applies personally as well as Cosmically) and shall reward every man according to his activity. The personal application is brought out when He says, "There be some standing here, which shall not taste of death till they see the Son of man coming in his kingdom". This means that the Christ Consciousness will spiritualize certain of the faculties—that they shall not "die" to the things of the flesh until they are contacted by this Christ Consciousness. It was also literally true that some of the Disciples saw Christ in all His glory before they passed on. The coming of Christ again will also be true Cosmically. From another angle, the Cosmic Christ Spirit ascends yearly to the Father and comes again in His glory to this earth, which is an annual Cosmic event. Although not seen by the masses, the influence is clearly felt, especially at Christmas time.

CHAPTER 17.

"And after six days Jesus taketh Peter, James, and John his brother, and bringeth them up into a high mountain apart, And was transfigured before them: and his face did shine as the sun, and his raiment was white as the light. And, behold, there appeared unto them Moses and Elias talking with him. Then answered Peter, and said unto Jesus, Lord, it is good for us to be here: if thou wilt, let us make here three tabernacles; one for thee, and one for Moses, and one for Elias. While he yet spake, behold a bright cloud overshadowed them: and behold a voice out of the cloud which said, This is my beloved Son in whom I am well pleased; hear ye him. And when the disciples heard it, they fell on their face, and were sore afraid. And Jesus came and touched them and said, Arise, and be not afraid. And when they had lifted up their eyes, they saw no man, save Jesus only. And as they came down from the mountain, Jesus charged them, saying, Tell the vision to no man, until the Son of man be risen again from the dead. And his disciples asked him, saying, Why then say these scribes that Elias must first come? And Jesus answered and said unto them, Elias truly shall first come, and restore all things. But I say unto you, That Elias is come already, and they knew him not, but have done unto him whatsoever they listed. Likewise shall also the Son of man suffer of them. Then the disciples understood that he spake unto them of John the Baptist".

The six days represent six stages in human evolution. The Christ vibration, at a not too distant future, will carry humanity to the high point known as the "Transfiguration". Again the mountain represents a great spiritual plane or place of Initiation. When they saw Moses and Elias, it was indicated that they were reading in the Memory of Nature, or that plane in which past records are stored. The same Ego or Spirit which incarnated as Moses was also Elias and later, John the Baptist. It is likely that Christ was tracing in the Memory of Nature the lives of this great teacher for the benefit of His Disciples. The manifestation of divinity, in the voice which spoke to Christ, frightened the three Disciples apparently, and they thus lost contact with this spiritual plane. They were all in confusion regarding Moses, Elias and John until the Christ explained Rebirth to them. He told them that Elias had come to birth in the person of John the Baptist and had been beheaded.

At a certain time on the path of attainment we are taught that the neophyte has the doctrine of Rebirth proven to him by watching an Ego lose its body in death (as a child) and take another body some years later.

The injunction, to "tell the vision to no man until the Son of man be risen again from the dead", may be a repetition of an occult law in order to impress it firmly on our minds. This is another way of stating, "When you are digging for treasure, a spoken word will cause it to disappear", which means that we have raised the higher self from a "dead" or dormant condition in the body to one of activity. We are taught that to relate or boast of our psychic experiences will prevent our attainment of Initiation. The Initiate must learn to hold his tongue. We are told that one of the maxims of an Initiate is, "To do, to dare and to remain silent".

"And when they were come to the multitude, there came to him a certain man, kneeling down to him, and saying, Lord, have mercy on my son: for he is lunatick, and sore vexed: for oftimes he falleth into the fire, and oft into the water. And I brought him to thy disciples, and they could not cure him. Then Jesus answered and said, O faithless and perverse generation, how long shall I be with you? how long shall I suffer you? bring him hither to me. And Jesus rebuked the devil; and he departed out of him: and the child was cured from that very hour. Then came the disciples to Jesus apart, and said, Why could not we cast him out? And Jesus said unto them, Because of your unbelief: for verily I say unto you, If ye have faith as a grain of mustard seed, ye shall say unto this mountain, Remove hence to yonder place; and it shall remove; and nothing shall be impossible unto you. Howbeit this kind goeth not out but by prayer and fasting".

The son represents the mind, particularly that newer phase of mind which has developed since the fall into generation. It is "lunatick" because it is "ill" and will only become "well" when we live according to Cosmic law. "Falling into the fire" describes the suffering as a result of the abuse of the creative force. "Falling into the water" represents the misuse of the emotional nature. Christ gives a very valuable hint to the neophyte when He says, "Howbeit this kind goeth not out but by prayer and fasting". This means that the mind is cleansed only through fasting and prayer. The Lord's Prayer is a scientific formula for building spiritual power. Fasting allows the Ego or Spirit to gain possession of the body and to acquire self-mastery through control of the blood. (For detailed information as to how this is done, read "Self-Mastery", one of the subjects in the booklet, "Occult Interpretations", by the author). We repeat that Christ, David, Elias, and other great Biblical characters fasted. We know that we could not do better than follow in the footsteps of the Christ. Fasting, however, with little knowledge concerning methods, etc. is very, very dangerous. We advise (from practical experience) the neophyte never to fast except under competent direction or with full knowledge himself of what he is doing.

"And while they abode in Galilee, Jesus said unto them, The son of man shall be betrayed into the hands of men: And they shall kill him, and the third day he shall be raised again. And they were exceeding sorry: And when they were come to Capernaum, they that received tribute money came to Peter and said, Doth not your master pay tribute? He saith, Yes. And when he was come into the house, Jesus prevented him saying, What thinkest thou, Simon? of whom do the kings of the earth take custom or tribute? of their own children, or of strangers? Peter saith unto him, Of strangers. Jesus saith unto him, Then are the children free. Notwithstanding, lest we should offend them, go thou to the sea, and cast an hook, and take up the fish that first cometh up; and when thou hast opened his mouth, thou shalt find a piece of money: that take, and give unto them for me and thee".

Cosmically, the betrayal of the Son of Man into the hands of men represents the light of the Ego being "dimmed" within the physical body. This is the same as the descent into material consciousness. The ego might be said to be "killed" in this process. The three days represent the three or three and a half great steps of our involutionary descent before we start back toward the "Father's home" again. The same idea is expressed in Masonry in the legend of the slaying of Hiram Abiff (the Spirit) by the "three ruffians", which are Lust, Pride and Selfishness. Being raised the third day indicates the raising of the "Master Mason" or the release of the Spirit from a materialistic condition. This is always accomplished in three steps. In Masonry these steps are the Entered Apprentice, Fellowcraft and Master degrees. In the Rosicrucian Fellowship they are the Student, Probationer and Disciple.

From the personal angle, the betrayal of the Son of Man represents the misuse of the spiritual force within the body by the lower faculties. "Truth crushed to earth shall rise again", and the Spirit within each of us is crucified many, many times before we finally learn to subdue the lower man.

The story of the tribute money signifies the fact that when we "cast a hook into the sea" and take up a "fish", we are raising above the waters of generation some brother or sister who has been living in the lower emotions. When they are "drawn up" above the "waters", wisdom (the gold coin) will be found in their mouths. They will then speak with that wisdom which comes to those who have attained self-mastery.

CHAPTER 18.

"At the same time came the disciples unto Jesus, saying. Who is the greatest in the kingdom of heaven? And Jesus called a little child unto him, and set him in the midst of them. And said, Verily I say unto you, Except ye be converted, and become as little children, ye shall not enter the kingdom of heaven. Whosoever therefore shall humble himself as this little child the same is greatest in the kingdom of heaven. And whoso shall receive one such little child in my name receiveth me. But whoso shall offend one of these little ones which believe in me, it were better for him that a millstone were hanged about his neck, and that he were drowned in the depth of the sea. Woe unto the world because of offences! for it must needs be that offences come; but woe to that man by whom the offence cometh!"

A little child has no predjudices nor preconceived opinions. Christ is stating a deep occult truth when He tells us that we must become as little children. The heaven worlds are different in many ways from what the masses conceive them to be. It is only when we become open-minded and capable of being taught like the little child that we can eliminate properly undesirable qualities and enter into the consciousness of higher planes. The person who thinks he already knows is incapable of being taught, and his pride of intellect will prevent his accepting new teachings.

The little child does not harbor such undesirable emotional and mental qualities as hatred, envy and jealousy, which act as barriers to spiritual advancement. A little child is simple and humble. Humility is one of the first traits the neophyte must cultivate. One cannot enter into the finer worlds without being humble.

Those who receive the little child (who is naturally Christ-like), receive the Christ, since the child possesses Christ-like qualities. It is better to drown in the "sea" of the lower emotions than to lead astray those who follow the Christ. "Offences" must come to try and test us and help us to convert innocence into virtue. Woe to that one who allows himself to play the part of the tempter, since the law of Cause and Effect decrees that he must pay in full for any injury that may ensue from his every act which may bring harm to another.

"Wherefore if thy hand or thy foot offend thee, cut them off, and cast them from thee: it is better for thee to enter into life halt or maimed, rather than having two hands or two feet to be cast into everlasting fire. And if thine eye offend thee, pluck it out, and cast it from thee: it is better for thee to enter into life with one eye, rather than having two eyes to be cast into hell fire".

Here we are warned that through one of the physical senses our whole body and mind may be caused to sin. It is better not to let one part of us cause the whole of us to sin and be destroyed. One rotten apple in a barrel can spoil a whole barrel of apples. We are, therefore, warned to guard each one of the physical senses and not to let one of them destroy us completely.

"Take heed that ye despise not one of these little ones; for I say unto you, That in heaven their angels do always behold the face of my Father which is in heaven".

We are taught that those who are not old enough to be accountable for their actions under the Law of Cause and Effect have a guardian angel. The penalty for harming someone who is not able to know the difference between right and wrong is, therefore, very severe.

"For the Son of man is come to save that which was lost. How think ye? if a man have an hundred sheep, and one of them be gone astray, doth he not leave the ninety and nine, and goeth into the mountains, and seeketh that which is gone astray? And if so be that he find it, verily I say unto you, he rejoiceth more of that sheep, than of the ninety and nine which went not astray. Even so it is not the will of your Father which is in heaven, that one of these little ones should perish".

In the personal sense, Christ tells us that He is come to save those "sheep" or those spiritual qualities which we had lost during our descent into the material world. "Sheep" symbolizes innocence or purity. Therefore, the individual who loses one of his "sheep" or one of his pure qualities, must go into the "mountain", a more advanced plane of consciousness, and there search to "find" or regain this lost quality. There is great rejoicing in his heart when he regains this lost spiritual faculty. This story is similar to the one of the woman who loses the coin and finally finds it. Christ says that it is not the will of the Father that even the least of the spiritual faculties or qualities shall be lost.

"Moreover if thy brother shall trespass against thee, go and tell him his fault between thee and him alone: if he shall hear thee, thou hast gained thy brother. But if he will not hear thee, then take with thee one or two more, that in the mouth of two or three witnesses every word may be established. And if he shall neglect to hear them tell it unto the church: but if he neglect to hear the church, let him be unto thee as an heathen man and a publican. Verily I say unto you, Whatsoever ye shall bind on earth shall be bound in heaven: and whatsoever ye shall loose on earth shall be loosed in heaven".

These verses emphasize the fact that the laws of heaven operate on earth; and that the activities of earth have their effects in the heaven worlds. Thus, if we save our brother and show him the working of Cosmic Law that he may use this for his benefit, we have "gained" him and he will also be "saved" on the higher planes when he passes on in death. What we "bind" on earth describes those qualities which we restrict or "bind". They will still be "bound" when we pass on to the higher planes and will not cause us misery in Purgatory. What we "loose" may be taken two ways. If we "loose" or cut adrift from those weights which hamper us at present, or if we free ourselves from sin in this world, we shall be free from the suffering caused by this hereafter. But if we "loose" our passions and lower desires and let them run wild in the physical world, they will also be "loose" or out of control when we pass on. This will cause us great misery.

"Again I say unto you, That if two of you shall agree on earth as touching any thing that they shall ask, it shall be done for them of my Father which is in heaven. For where two or three are gathered together in my name, there am I in the midst of them".

We know the power of thought and particularly the power of massed concentration. Each additional person who prays in unison multiplies the power in bringing down the Christ Force. It is literally true that when two or three pray together, they can bring down from higher realms an actual power. Esoterically, this may mean that where the mind and the heart (the two poles of being) get together or both seek Christ, He will be there with them.

"Then came Peter to him, and said Lord, how oft shall my brother sin against me, and I forgive him? till seven times? Jesus saith unto him, I say not unto thee, Until seven times: but, Until seventy times seven. Therefore is the kingdom of heaven likened unto a certain king, which would take account of his servants. And when he had begun to reckon, one was brought unto him, which owed him ten thousand talents. But forasmuch as he had not to pay, his lord commanded him to be sold and his wife, and children, and all that he had, and payment to be made. The servant therefore fell down, and worshipped him, saying Lord, have patience with me, and I will pay thee all. Then the Lord of that servant was moved with compassion, and loosed him, and forgave him the debt. But the same servant went out and found one of his fellowservants, which owed him an hundred pence: and he laid hands on him, and took him by the throat, saying, Pay me that thou owest. And his fellowservant fell down at his feet, and besought him, saying,

Have patience with me, and I will pay thee all. And he would not: but went and cast him into prison, till he should pay the debt. So when his fellowservants saw what was done, they were very sorry, and came and told unto their lord all that was done. Then his lord, after that he had called him, said unto him, O thou wicked servant, I forgave thee all that debt, because thou desiredst me: Shouldest not thou also have had compassion on thy fellowservant, even as I had pity on thee? And his lord was wroth, and delivered him to the tormentors, till he should pay all that was due unto him. So likewise shall my heavenly Father do also unto you, if ye from your hearts forgive not every one his brother their trespasses".

Again, both the forgiveness of sin, which comes through the Christ, and the Mosaic Law of Cause and Effect are taught us. Both work scientifically and impartially in our lives. It is the law that what we send out comes back to us. It is the law of Christ that when we ask forgiveness and truly repent, our sins are forgiven us. But it is also the law that if we do not forgive others, we cannot be forgiven ourselves, since the law of Moses would prevent it.

In this somewhat complicated story, we are told that the Christ law of love and the law of Jehovah or form both work at the same time in connection with the law of Cause and Effect. Let us all pray that we will always keep the laws of God in mind and build them within, so that we may not live contrary to them and thereby bring down the automatic reactions upon ourselves, as a result of breaking them. Let us pray that we may live in harmony with them and benefit by their divine working.

CHAPTER 19.

"And it came to pass, that when Jesus had finished these sayings, he departed from Galilee, and came into the coasts of Judæa beyond Jordan; And great multitudes followed him; and he healed them there. The Pharisees also came to him, tempting him, and saying unto him, Is it lawful for a man to put away his wife for every cause, And he answered and said unto them, Have ye not read, that he which made them at the beginning made them male and female, And said, For this cause shall a man leave father and mother, and shall cleave to his wife: and they twain shall be one flesh? Wherefore they are no more twain, but one flesh. What God hath joined together, let not man put asunder. They say unto him, why did Moses then command to give a writing of divorcement, and to put her away? He saith unto them, Moses because of the hardness of your hearts suffered you to put away your wives: but from the beginning it was not so.

And I say unto you, Whosoever shall put away his wife, except it be for fornication, and shall marry another, committeth adultery: and whoso marrieth her which is put away doth commit adultery. His disciples say unto him, If the case of the man be so with his wife, it is not good to marry. But he said unto them, All men cannot receive this saying, save they to whom it is given. For there are some eunuchs, which were so born from their mother's womb: and there are some eunuchs, which were made eunuchs of men: and there be eunuchs, which have made themselves eunuchs for the kingdom of heaven's sake. He that is able to receive it, let him receive it".

Christ tells us that, "It was different in the beginning". He may be referring to the time in the beginning of our involutionary journey when we were dual-sexed and did not require the help of another being in order to generate a new physical body. It was a law of Moses that a man must give his wife a bill of divorcement before divorcing her, which shows that things were done according to form under the regime of Jehovah. With the coming of Christ a better understanding of the law is given. This explanation takes into consideration the occult fact that in marriage there is an actual blending of the blood of the man and his wife. Consequently, it is not right that the vital bodies of men and women be blended indiscriminately. It is necessary to know something about this vital body (see "Cosmo-Conception") in order to understand how this blending of the blood is accomplished through the marriage act.

Therefore, according to the Bible, adultery should be the only cause for divorce, as the marriage partner who commits adultery is really violating a Cosmic law. This is sure to cause disharmony between the person and the marriage partner.

Those who make themselves "eunuchs" for the kingdom of heaven's sake are those who retain their seed and absorb it within the being to illuminate the "temple of God", which is the body. They are the ones who become saints and who truly teach the word of God. May the time come when we will all become "eunuchs", except when children are to be brought into the world, as this is the purpose of the creative function. May we all live lives of purity so there may be "peace on earth and good will toward men", with no more depressions or other undesirable conditions which show the result of greed or lust on the part of those who are not spiritual "eunuchs".

"Then were there brought unto him little children, that he should put his hands on them, and pray: and the disciples rebuked them. But Jesus said, Suffer little children, and forbid them not, to come unto me: for of such is the kingdom of heaven. And he laid his hands on them, and departed thence. And, behold, one came and said unto him, Good Master, what good thing shall I do, that I may have eternal life? And he said unto him, Why callest thou me good? there is none good but one, that is, God: but if thou wilt enter into life, keep the commandments. He saith unto him, Which? Jesus said, Thou shalt do no murder, Thou shalt not commit adultery, Thou shalt not steal, Thou shalt not bear false witness. Honor thy father and thy mother: and, Thou shalt love thy neighbour as thyself. The young man saith unto him, All these things have I kept from my youth up: what lack I yet? Jesus said unto him, If thou wilt be perfect go and sell that thou hast, and give to the poor, and thou shalt have treasure in heaven: and come and follow me. But when the young man heard that saying, he went away sorrowful: for he had great possessions Then said Jesus unto his disciples, Verily I say unto you, That a rich man shall hardly enter into the kingdom of heaven. And again I say unto you, It is easier for a camel to go through the eye of a needle, than for a rich man to enter into the kingdom of God. When his disciples heard it, they were exceedingly amazed, saying, Who then can be saved? But Jesus beheld them, and said unto them, With men this is impossible; but with God all things are possible. Then answered Peter and said unto him, Behold, we have forsaken all, and followed thee; what shall we have therefore? And Jesus said unto them, Verily I say unto you, that ye which have followed me, in the regeneration when the Son of man shall sit in the throne of his glory, ye also shall sit upon twelve thrones, judging the twelve tribes of Israel. And every one that hath forsaken houses, or brethren, or sisters, or father, or mother, or wife, or children, or lands, for my name's sake, shall receive an hundredfold, and shall inherit everlasting life. But many that are first shall be last; and the last shall be first".

We are again shown that we must attain certain of the qualities of a child before we can come into a purer consciousness. We are also shown, in the case of the rich young man, that the mere keeping of the law is not sufficient. That was the old form of religion. Now we must come into the realization that our very lives belong to God. Justification is the first step, but consecration must be the next. We must realize that we are but the stewards of our earthly possessions. The very atoms of our physical bodies are used to form other bodies after our death. The love of riches is one of the greatest hindrances on the spiritual path. This is well-illustrated in the case of the rich young man who refused to put Christ above his earthly possessions. This is one of the first tests of the neophyte.

The "eye of the needle" was a certain gate leading into Jerusalem. It was possible for a camel to pass through this gate, but in order to do so, his pack had to be taken off and he was forced to get down on his knees and crawl through. Just so will the rich man be forced to remove his pride of wealth and humble himself in order to enter into the kingdom of heaven.

The Disciples are told by Christ that when they have regenerated themselves and the Christ Within is glorified, they shall each rule the "twelve tribes of Israel" or the twelve attributes within themselves. The real self, the Spirit, will be the ruler.

In the next to the last verse it is not intended that Man should break any obligations in regard to mothers, fathers, sisters, brothers, houses, etc. It is intended that Man must recognize these kin people as bodies of indwelling Spirits. They are to be forsaken in the narrow, selfish, clannish spirit but accepted in the broader spirit in which the kinship is not limited to those of mere blood relationship. Until we forsake the narrow, clannish relationship for that of the broader spiritual relationship, we shall make little progress on the Path.

Many who are considered first in the physical world shall be the last in the spiritual. This also refers to the Spirit or Ego, which was our first manifestation within the Being of God and which shall be last, or shall endure after the physical man is a thing of the past.

CHAPTER 20.

"For the kingdom of heaven is like unto a man that is an householder, which went out early in the morning to hire labourers into his vineyard. And when he had agreed with the labourers for a penny a day, he sent them into his vineyard. And he went out about the third hour, and saw others standing in the market place, And said unto them; Go ye also into the vineyard, and whatsoever is right I will give you. And they went their way. Again he went out about the sixth and the ninth hour; and did likewise. And about the eleventh hour he went out, and found others standing idle, and saith unto them, Why stand ye here all the day idle? They say unto him, Because no man hath hired us. He saith unto them, Go ye also into the vineyard; and whatsoever is right, that shall ye receive. So when the even was come, the lord of the vineyard saith unto his steward, Call the labourers and give them their hire, beginning from the last unto the first. And when they came that were hired about the eleventh hour, they received every man a penny. But when the first came, they supposed that they should have received more; and they likewise received every man a penny. And when they had received it, they murmured against the goodman of the house, Saying, These last have wrought but one hour, and thou hast made them equal unto us, which have borne the burden and heat of the day. But he answered one of them, and said, Friend, I do thee no wrong: didst not thou agree with me for a penny? Take that thine is, and go thy way: I will give unto this last, even as unto thee. Is it not lawful for me to do what I will with mine own? Is thine eye evil, because I am good? So the last shall be first, and the first last: for many be called, but few chosen".

The labourers in the vineyard represent those who carry out the will of God. The wages given them are in the form of personal development. The pioneer who works constructively must realize that his reward will be the work accomplished and his own individual development and not greater possessions than another. Those who work spiritually for the purpose of attaining an advantage over their fellow men shall be doomed to disappointment, since we will have all things in common in the kingdom of heaven. The occult statement, "the last shall be first and the first last", applies to many phases of both personal and Cosmic development. As one example, the female sex organ was first developed and will be the last of the two to atrophy. Another example is that the first or highest-ranking individual in the material world will be last in the heaven worlds. Many of the last to be regarded physically will be among the first or highest spiritually. The "many who are called" are the many to whom the Gospel is preached. The "few who are chosen" are the few who choose to live the spiritual life. They automatically become "chosen" because they first choose God, and because they become qualified to do more advanced work than the masses.

"And Jesus going up to Jerusalem took the twelve disciples apart in the way, and said unto them, Behold, we go up to Jerusalem; and the Son of man shall be betrayed unto the chief priests and unto the scribes, and they shall condemn him to death, And shall deliver him to the Gentiles to mock, and to scourge, and to crucify him: and the third day he shall rise again. Then came to him the mother of Zebedee's children with her sons, worshipping him, and desiring a certain thing of him. And he said unto her, what wilt thou? She saith unto him, Grant that these my two sons may sit, the one on thy right hand, and the other on the left, in thy kingdom. But Jesus answered and said, Ye know not what ye ask. Are ye able to drink of the cup that I shall drink of, and to be baptized with the baptism that I am baptized with? They say unto him, We are able. And he saith unto them, Ye shall drink indeed of my cup, and be baptized with the baptism that I am baptized with: but to sit on my right hand, and on my left, is not mine to give, but it shall be given to them for whom it is prepared of my Father. And when the ten heard it, they were moved with indignation against the two brethren. But Jesus called them unto him, and said, Ye know that the princes of the Gentiles exercise dominion over them, and they that are great exercise authority upon them. But it shall not be so among you: but whosoever will be great among you, let him be your minister; And whosoever will be chief among you, let him be your servant: Even as the Son of man came not to be ministered unto, but to minister, and to give his life a ransom for many".

The journey of Christ to Jerusalem represents the ascent of the Spirit to the "dome" of the "temple"—the head. That the Disciples also went with Him shows that the twelve faculties within also become spiritualized and come under the rulership of the Christ Within. The chief priests and the scribes are the cold mental phases of being which are incapable of appreciating the warmth of the Christ Love-Wisdom principle, and they condemn it. Being delivered to the "Gentiles" is being delivered to the "uncircumcised" or unspiritualized phases of the being—those phases which are opposed to the Spirit. It is a fact that each one of us "crucifies" the Christ Within every day of our lives. Meditate on this. His rising on the third day indicates the completion of the third step in our spiritual development when we become true "Master Masons" or Initiates.

We may all drink of the "cup" which Christ drank of if we only will. This "cup" is the "sacrament cup" in the body, from which we must "drink" if we are to regenerate our bodies. This process results in the "baptism" of the Holy Spirit, which is the drawing down to us of the divine power of God.

Christ saw that the Disciples did not understand His status as a great spiritual being, leader of the Archangels, which is two great steps above humanity. The Disciples believed Christ to be a man like themselves. Only later did they understand fully that the physical body was that of the high Initiate, Jesus, who had given it to the Christ Spirit in which to function. They eventually learned to see beyond the physical body of Jesus and to know of the great Being who inhabited it for the three years of his ministry. Consequently, in their ignorance, they asked of Him something much greater than they realized, to sit at the right hand of the great Spirit who had raised His consciousness from that of an Archangel to the throne of the Father.

Christ tells us that the one who profits most spiritually is he who serves the best. Spiritual advancement is dependent upon this service. This is the meaning of, "Let him who would be the greatest among you be the servant of all". This Christ practiced Himself, because during His life on earth He served all of humanity and attained the greatest name of any who have ever walked our earth.

"And as they departed from Jerico, a great multitude followed him. And, behold, two blind men sitting by the way side, when they heard that Jesus passed by, cried out, saying, Have mercy on us, O Lord, thou son of David. And the multitude rebuked them, because they should hold their peace: but they cried the more, saying, Have mercy on us, O Lord, thou son of David. And Jesus stood still, and called them, and said, What will ye that I shall do unto you? They say unto him, Lord, that our eyes may be opened. So Jesus had compassion on them, and touched their eyes: and immediately their eyes received sight, and they followed him".

We are all, spiritually, "blind men" sitting by the side of the "Road of Life". When the Christ Force passes along the spinal canal on the way to "Jerusalem", it shall open our spiritual "eyes" and we shall "see". That part of our being represented by the multitude "rebukes" those phases of us which call on the Christ Within, since it is the "multitude" or "people" which crucify the Christ. If we are persistent in calling on the Christ Within, not forgetting at the same time to work and not be idle, He will cure our spiritual illnesses and give us spiritual sight in place of spiritual "blindness".

CHAPTER 21.

"And when they drew nigh unto Jerusalem, and were come to Bethphage, unto the mount of Olives, then sent Jesus two disciples, Saying unto them, Go into the village over against you, and straightway ye shall find an ass tied, and a colt with her: loose them, and bring them unto me. And if any man say ought unto you, ye shall say, The Lord hath need of them; and straightway he will send them. All this was done, that it might be fulfilled which was spoken by the prophet, saying, Tell ye the daughter of Sion, Behold, Thy King cometh unto thee, meek and sitting upon an ass, and a colt the foal of an ass. And the disciples went, and did as Jesus commanded them, And brought the ass, and the colt, and put on them their clothes, and they set him thereon. And a very great multitude spread their garments in the way; others cut down branches from the trees, and strawed them in the way. And the multitude that went before, and that followed, cried, saying, Hosanna to the son of David: Blessed is he that cometh in the name of the Lord; Hosanna in the highest".

The Disciples who are sent to get the ass represent two of the faculties which are instrumental in raising the Spinal Fire from that region of the body where it is found, up to the solar plexus, where the Christ Within uses it to "carry" Him on up the spinal canal. This Force carries the Christ Within up to the head, represented by Jerusalem. When this is accomplished, the whole consciousness rejoices. In other words, the above verses describe the Spinal Spirit Fire ascending from the cardia to the pineal gland and pituitary body. It is a time of great rejoicing for the neophyte because clairvoyance and clairaudience result from this step.

"And when he was come into Jerusalem, all the city was moved, saying, Who is this? And the multitude said, This is Jesus the prophet of Nazareth of Galilee. And Jesus went into the temple of God, and cast out all them that sold and bought in the temple, and overthrew the tables of the moneychangers, and the seats of them that sold doves. And said unto them, It is written, My house shall be called the house of prayer; but ye have made it a den of thieves. And the blind and the lame came to him in the temple; and he healed them. And when the chief priests and scribes saw the wonderful things that he did, and the children crying in the the temple, and saying, Hosanna to the son of David; they were sore displeased, And said unto him, Hearest thou what these say? And Jesus saith unto them, Yea; have ye never read, Out of the mouth of babes and sucklings thou hast perfected praise?"

Jerusalem symbolizes the "dome" of the "temple" and also the higher consciousness. This is naturally influenced or "moved" when the Christ Force reaches it, borne on the "back" of what had been the animal force within the body. The casting out of the moneychangers and the sellers of doves from the temple is the "casting out" of those lower attributes which add to the materialistic consciousness of the person. The "moneychangers" are those which tend to make the Spirit subservient to the material phase of self, as do the "sellers of doves", since a dove symbolizes purity. Thus, one who "sells doves" is one who exchanges purity for any material gain.

The body is truly intended to be a temple, "a house of prayer", because our daily lives should be a constant prayer. Through many sinful acts, however, we have made the body a "den of theives". The many materialistic qualities within us "steal" the time and thought that should be devoted to the spiritual life.

The healing of the lame and blind has already been explained several times.

The children crying in the temple are the "young" or new faculties which are always born as a result of the Christ influence in the "temple" or body. These new spiritual faculties "cry out" in gladness and joy. The chief priests and scribes represent the purely mental and form type of religion, which neither understands nor appreciates the things of the Spirit. Christ says that these new faculties (children) express a higher and purer spirit than the more sophisticated phases of being.

"And he left them, and went out of the city into Bethany; and he lodged there. Now in the morning as he returned into the city he hungered. And when he saw a fig tree in the way, he came to it, and found nothing thereon, but leaves only, and said unto it, Let no fruit grow on thee henceforward for ever. And presently the fig tree withered away. And when the disciples saw it, they marvelled, saying How soon is the fig tree withered away! Jesus answered and said unto them, Verily I say unto you, If ye have faith, and doubt not, ye shall not only do this which is done unto this fig tree, but also if ye shall say unto this mountain, Be thou removed, and be thou cast into the sea; it shall be done. And all things, whatsoever ye shall ask in prayer, believing ye shall receive".

A city always indicates a state of consciousness. Bethany means "a house of dates" and represents fruitfulness. We must remember that the Bible is a spiritual book, and therefore, hunger and food are usually representative of spiritual hunger and spiritual food. Each of us becomes spiritually hungry when we "lodge" in the state of consciousness of "Bethany" or when we become fruitful and begin to produce in a spiritual manner.

A fig tree signifies productiveness. In this connection, it indicates the same "tree" from which Adam and Eve ate the apple. The figs represent spiritual "fruit" or that part of the Life Force used for the purpose of regeneration. Christ did not literally curse the fig tree, but was merely stating a fact. This fact is that the Life Force which is used sensually, in generation and degeneration, does not produce "fruit" in a spiritual sense. The gratification of sensual desire is certainly not spiritual productiveness. Furthermore, if we do not produce the "figs" of regeneration within ourselves upon our "fig trees", the "fig tree" will wither away and become incapable of producing spiritual fruit. This is because all of its strength will have been wasted physically. When it is said that only the "leaves" were on the "tree" and no "fruit", it may indicate that great groups of people who appear spiritual but in secret do not live the life.

Removing the mountain into the sea represents the cleansing of the desire nature. The "sea" represents the emotional nature and the mountain symbolizes a high state of consciousness. Consequently, having the faith to remove a "mountain" into the "sea" may indicate the raising of the emotions to a higher, purer level.

"And all things, whatsoever ye shall ask in prayer, etc." refers to spiritual things, for the Bible is a spiritual book. It is an occult truth that we must have faith if we wish to have our prayers answered.

"And when he was come into the temple, the chief priests and the elders of the people came unto him as he was teaching, and said, By what authority doest thou these things? and who gave thee this authority? And Jesus answered and said unto them, I also will ask you one thing, which if ye tell me, I in like wise will tell you by what authority I do these things. The baptism of John, whence was it? from heaven or of men? And they reasoned within themselves, saying, If we shall say, From heaven: he will say unto us, Why did ye not then believe him? But if we shall say, Of men: we fear the people; for all hold John as a prophet. And they answered Jesus, and said, We cannot tell. And he said unto them, Neither tell I you by what authority I do these things.

The critical faculties of the mind, represented by the scribes and elders, seek to find fault with the Christ Within, and consequently, are utterly incapable of understanding spiritual truths.

The baptizing done by John was both physical and spiritual if the applicant was truly ready for "baptism". The scribes and elders were not capable of seeing beyond the physical symbol, and so did not comprehend the question of the Christ. If a person being baptized truly repented of his sins and raised himself above the "waters" of generation, in time this regenerative process brought down the "baptism" of the Spirit. Consequently, they would receive a spiritual "baptism" as a result of a physical one. Some who were ready brought down the spiritual down-pouring even at the time of the physical baptism. It is naturally the spiritual "baptism" that is to be sought. The physical baptism is but a symbol of the regenerative process.

"But what think ye? A certain man had two sons; and he came to the first, and said, Son, go to work today in my vineyard. He answered and said, I will not: but afterward he repented, and went. And he came to the second, and said likewise. And he answered and said, I go, sir, and went not. Whether of them twain did the will of his father? They say unto him, The first. Jesus saith unto them, Verily I say unto you, That the publicans and the harlots go into the kingdom of God before you. For John came unto you in the way of righteousness, and ye believed him not: but the publicans and the harlots believed him: and ye, when ye had seen it, repented not afterward, that ye might believe him".

The two sons represent the two principle types of individuals, the head or mental type, and the heart or emotional type. The heart type (the harlots and publicans) may at first refuse to "work in the vineyard" or lead a constructive life in the world. However, they usually repent of their sins and turn to God after having been enlightened. The head type, representing the person whose religion is one of form and who worships only with his mind, agrees in words to live a constructive life, but since it is only on the surface, he never really enters into the spirit of the work. Thus, we see that the "harlots" and "publicans" who repent and receive the Christ into their hearts will much sooner reach enlightenment than the cold head type.

"Who walks the path alone to save his soul,
   May keep the path but will not reach the goal.
Who walks the path of Love may wander far,
   But God will bring him where the blessed are."

"Hear another parable: There was a certain householder, which planted a vineyard, and hedged it round about, and digged a winepress in it, and built a tower, and let it out to husbandmen, and went into a far country: And when the time of the fruit drew near, he sent his servants to the husbandmen, that they might receive the fruits of it. And the husbandmen took his servants, and beat one, and killed another, and stoned another. Again, he sent other servants more than the first: and they did unto them likewise. But last of all he sent unto them his son, saying, They will reverence my son. But when the husbandmen saw the son they said among themselves, This is the heir; come, let us kill him, and let us seize on his inheritance. And they caught him and slew him. When the lord therefore of the vineyard cometh, what will he do unto those husbandmen? They say unto him, He will miserably destroy those wicked men, and will let out his vineyard unto other husbandmen which shall render him the fruits in their seasons. Jesus saith unto them, Did ye never read in the scriptures. The stone which the builders rejected, the same is become the head of the corner: this is the Lord's doing, and it is marvellous in our eyes? Therefore say I unto you, The kingdom of God shall be taken from you, and given to a nation bringing forth the fruits thereof. And whosoever shall fall on this stone shall be broken: but on whomsoever it shall fall, it will grind him to powder. And when the chief priests and Pharisees had heard his parables, they perceived that he spake of them. But when they sought to lay hands on him, they feared the multitude, because they took him for a prophet".

In the personal sense, the vineyard may represent the individual physical body, which constitutes a little world of itself, as well as being part of the outer physical world. The "winepress" is the seat of the Life Force and the "tower" the brain. We, as Egos or "husbandmen", occupy this "vineyard". In the beginning of our evolution we descended from the finer spiritual worlds and consequently lost direct contact with God. This is the meaning (one meaning) of the owner of the vineyard journeying into a far country. We do not give God the "fruits" of our vineyard and even "kill" the Christ Within or the "Son".

According to another interpretation, it is plainly evident that the world is a "vineyard" and we are the "husbandmen" who have rejected the servants of God who came to us. Finally, the Christ Himself is sent to us. He is rejected and crucified. The people to whom He was particularly sent were the Jewish people, who at one time were part of the "chosen ones" of God. They were "chosen" to form a new race, but disobeyed God and married into inferior races. Today their place has been taken by the Anglo-Saxon-Teutonic races. Unless the Jewish people amalgamate with them in the formation of the next root race, they will become laggards in evolution and will be a lost race. Of course, any individual among them may always regain his status if he exerts himself sufficiently and there is enough time.

The "stone which the builders rejected" is, of course, the Christ, who must be the "head stone" of our individual "church" within as well as the "corner stone". The only physical edifice having a head stone which also serves as a corner stone is the Great Pyramid. The word Pyramid means "measure of light". It is noteworthy that the head stone has never been placed on the Pyramid. This may symbolize the fact that Christ has never been completely accepted. When either a nation or an individual truly accepts the Christ, its spiritual structure will become complete. The Pyramid represents the human body in the personal interpretation. The new American dollar now bears the picture of the Great Pyramid. It may be that this is a symbol given by the spiritual powers to us to tell us that we must, both individually and as a nation, complete the spiritual "Pyramid" by placing the Christ as the "head" and "corner stone" at the apex of our being. Each time we handle one of these bills, certain impressions will be received, whether we realize it or not. The placing of the Pyramid on the American dollar indicates that the United States must become a Christian nation in spirit as it has become one in form.

Whoever shall "fall" on the "stone" of Christ, or that person to whom the Christ is an offence, shall indeed be "broken", for it is only by accepting the Christ that we become alive and walk in the light. The one upon whom this Christ Force "falls" by violating His laws, will be ground into the "powder" of death spiritually and physically.

CHAPTER 22.

"And Jesus answered and spake unto them again by parables, and said. The kingdom of heaven is like unto a certain king, which made a marriage for his son. And sent forth his servants to call them that were bidden to the wedding: and they would not come. Again he sent forth other servants, saying, Tell them which are bidden, Behold I have prepared my dinner: my oxen and my fatlings are killed, and all things are ready: come unto the marriage. But they made light of it, and went their ways, one to his farm, another to his merchandise: And the remnant took his servants, and entreated them spitefully, and slew them. But when the king heard thereof, he was wroth: and he sent forth his armies, and destroyed those murderers, and burned up their city. Then saith he to his servants, The wedding is ready, but they that were bidden are not worthy. Go ye therefore in the highways, and as many as ye shall find, bid to the marriage. So those servants went out into the highways, and gathered together all as many as they found, both bad and good: and the wedding was furnished with guests. And when the king came in to see the guests, he saw there a man which had not on a wedding garment: And he saith unto him, Friend, how camest thou in hither not having a wedding garment? And he was speechless. Then said the king to the servants, Bind him hand and foot, and take him away, and cast him into outer darkness; there shall be weeping and gnashing of teeth. For many are called, but few are chosen".

The king, of course, represents God the Father and his son represents the Christ. The "wedding" is the second coming of Christ, which we are all looking for. This will be the "marriage" of the "Bridegroom" to his "bride", the church. The servants represent the spiritual teachers or prophets who try to induce the people to accept the Christ and thus acquire the state of consciousness necessary to take part in the "wedding". After these prophets, God sends other teachers, but still the people mistreat those who come to them with the higher teachings of the Christ. They refuse to listen to the law of Love. It is beyond their comprehension. Kindly notice that the higher teachings are first sent to the invited "guests" or chosen people, who are in the front rank of evolution. Later it is given to those in the "highways" of Life, the masses of humanity.

The armies which the king sends to destroy those who have mistreated and killed his servants, symbolize the spiritual beings and forces which automatically destroy those who oppose the laws of God. By the word "destroy" we do not mean that the spiritual part of the man is destroyed, since that is immortal. It is only the vehicles of the Spirit which are destroyed. When this happens the Spirit becomes "naked" and must drop out of the present school of evolution to begin again at another later period. It is a very great and serious thing for the Spirit to drop back into another school of evolution.

After the select few to whom the teachings are given refuse to accept them, they are given to the entire world, or those in the "highways". This is a hint to the pioneers of evolution that if they do not continue to progress they will lose their present status as "chosen ones". When this happens, the lesser races, the laggards in evolution or those in the "highways" of life, may arrive at the "wedding feast" before them.

After everyone is gathered at the wedding, the king sees that one man does not have on a wedding garment. Apparently without any justice, this poor man who did not have time to dress appropriately for the occasion is thrown out into the night. The explanation of this is that all during life we are being exhorted by God's servants to prepare ourselves and build the "wedding garment" or soul body in which we are to be caught up in the air to meet the Christ at His second coming. It is perfectly just that the person who does not live a spiritual life, and thus build the spiritual vehicle necessary to function in the air, will automatically, as the Bible teaches, be cast into "outer darkness". He will not be able to "see" or know anything of the coming of the Saviour. He will be "tied" hand and foot through lack of a spiritual vehicle in which to function.

"Many are called, but few are chosen" means that the teaching of the Christ is given to many, but few will accept it and make it a part of their lives. Those who do accept it will have "chosen" God, and therefore will become "chosen" *of* God.

"Then went the Pharisees, and took counsel how they might entangle him in his talk. And they sent out unto him their disciples with the Herodians, saying, Master, we know that thou art true, and teachest the way of God in truth, neither carest thou for any man: for thou regardest not the person of men. Tell us therefore, What thinkest thou? Is it lawful to give tribute unto Cæsar, or not? But Jesus perceived their wickedness, and said, Why tempt ye me, ye hypocrites? Shew me the tribute money. And they brought unto him a penny. And he saith unto them, Whose is this image and superscription? They say unto him, Cæsar's Then saith he unto them, Render therefore unto Cæsar the things which are Cæsar's; and unto God the things that are God's. When they had heard these words, they marvelled, and left him, and went their way".

These verses bring out the same principles as the story of Mary and Martha. Cæsar, of course, represents our material obligations and duties. These must be fulfilled. Only when we have rendered what is due unto Cæsar or the material part of ourselves are we free to serve God. "Cæsar" includes the things of the body and of the material world which should not be neglected when we take up spiritual work, as do so many students. It will be impressed upon the reader more clearly what this lesson holds if we consider the country of India, where "Cæsar" receives a very small part of his due. Consequently, this country is very lacking in the sanitary and other necessary things of civilization. We are told that its people suffer greatly from disease and the masses live in a pitiful condition.

"The same day came to him the Sadducees, which say that there is no resurrection, and asked him, saying, Master, Moses said, if a man die, having no children, his brother shall marry his wife, and raise up his seed unto his brother. Now there were with us seven brethren: and the first, when he had married a wife, deceased, and, having no issue, left his wife unto his brother.: Likewise the second also, and the third, unto the seventh. And last of all the woman died also. Therefore in the resurrection whose wife shall she be of the seven? for they all had her. Jesus answered and said unto them, Ye do err, not knowing the scriptures, nor the power of God. For in the resurrection they neither marry, nor are given in marriage, but are as the angels of God in heaven. But as touching the resurrection of the dead, have ye not read that which was spoken unto you by God, saying, I am the God of Abraham, and the God of Isaac, and the God of Jacob? God is not the God of the dead, but of the living. And when the multitude heard this, they were astonished at his doctrine. But when the Pharisees had heard that he had put the Sadducees to silence, they were gathered together. Then one of them, which was a lawyer, asked him a question, tempting him, and saying, Master, which is the great commandment in the law?

Jesus said unto him, Thou shalt love the Lord thy God with all thy heart, and with all thy soul, and with all thy mind. This is the first and great commandment. And the second is like unto it, Thou shalt love thy neighbour as thyself. On these two commandments hang all the law and the prophets".

The story of the seven brethren and the one wife reveals to us that if we are to bring the "kingdom of heaven" consciousness into manifestation within ourselves, we must live the life that is lived in heaven. This will be a life without sex. This does not mean that we are not to bring children into the world. We must hold the ideal of bringing them into existence in a pure manner through a virgin birth, so they will have pure and healthy bodies.

When Christ says that God is the God of the living and not of the dead, He plainly implies that there are no dead, and that Abraham, Isaac and Jacob never died but simply passed on to another state of consciousness on other planes. Occult students know that there is no death except the dissolution of the physical body.

In these verses Christ gives the very heart of His teachings, which is the love of God and the love of Man. Those who love God love their fellow man, and those who carry out these commands, the other commandments will in time become a part of themselves. Love is the keynote of the Christ teachings.

"While the Pharisees were gathered together, Jesus asked them, Saying, What think ye of Christ? whose son is he? They say unto him, The son of David. He saith unto them, how then doth David in spirit call him Lord, saying, The Lord saith unto my Lord, Sit thou on my right hand, till I make thine enemies thy footstool? If David then call him Lord, how is he his son? And no man was able to answer him a word, neither durst any man from that day forth ask him any more questions".

In spiritual studies, we must not confuse physical things and spiritual things. Jesus was a man who was descended from David. Christ was a great spiritual being who had never before occupied a physical body. He took possession of the body of Jesus at the time of the Baptism, with the permission of Jesus. From that time on, Jesus functioned in the heaven worlds in a higher vehicle. The Christ Spirit used the body of Jesus for three years, from the Baptism to the Crucifixion. Christ also used the vital body of Jesus. (For detailed information, read the "Cosmo-Conception").

It is only when one studies the deeper philosophies that he is able to answer the questions put to the Pharisees by the Christ. This is a hint that if we wish to understand the deeper mysteries of the Spirit, we must go beyond a merely physical study of spiritual things.

CHAPTER 23.

"Then spake Jesus to the multitude, and to his disciples, Saying, The scribes and the Pharisees sit in Moses' seat: All therefore whatsoever they bid you observe, that observe and do; but do not ye after their works: for they say, and do not. For they bind heavy burdens and grevious to be borne, and lay them on men's shoulders; but they themselves will not move them with one of their fingers. But all their works they do for to be seen of men: they make broad their phylacteries, and enlarge the borders of their garments, And love the uppermost rooms at feasts, and the chief seats in the synagogues, And greetings in the markets, and to be called of men, Rabbi, Rabbi. But be not called Rabbi: for one is your Master, even Christ; and all ye are brethren. And call no man your father upon the earth: for one is your Father, which is in heaven. Neither be ye called master: for one is your Master, even Christ. But he that is greatest among you shall be your servant. And whosoever shall exalt himself shall be abased; and he that shall humble himself shall be exalted. But woe unto you, scribes and Pharisees, hypocrites! for ye shut up the kingdom of heaven against men: for ye neither go in yourselves, neither suffer ye them that are entering to go in. Woe unto you, scribes and Pharisees, hypocrites! for ye devour widows' houses, and for a pretence make long prayer: therefore ye shall receive the greater damnation. Woe unto you, scribes and Pharisees, hypocrites! for ye compass sea and land to make one proselyte, and when he is made, ye make him twofold more the child of hell than yourselves".

As previously mentioned, the scribes and Pharisees represent attributes of the mind which can never understand the true meaning of religion until they allow the heart to become spiritually active. When they sit in "Moses' seat", it is indicated that the understanding of spiritual law is only a mental one. The heart or intuitive side has not been awakened. These phases of the mind are cold, selfish, envious, puffed up and all the other things which St. Paul tells us Love is not. So we can see that such an understanding of spiritual law is not a correct one. Christ impresses us with the thought that the heart must not be neglected in religion, for the mind without the heart will lead us far astray from the Spirit. This is impressed upon us by the fact that the scribes and Pharisees (mental phases) tell others to do things but don't do them themselves. They lay heavy burdens on others; seek the high places at feasts and in synagogues; exalt themselves in pride; and while they observe the letter of the law, they are far from the spirit of it. Through their bad example, they even turn others away from spiritual work.

"'Woe unto you, ye blind guides, which say, Whosoever shall swear by the temple, it is nothing; but whosoever shall swear by the gold in the temple, he is a debtor! Ye fools and blind: for whether is greater, the gold, or the temple that sanctifieth the gold? And, Whosoever shall swear by the altar, it is nothing; but whosoever sweareth by the gift that is upon it, he is guilty. Ye fools and blind: for whether is greater, the gift, or the altar that sanctifieth the gift? Whoso therefore shall swear by the altar sweareth by it, and by all things thereon. And whoso shall swear by the temple, sweareth by it and by him that dwelleth therein. And he that shall swear by heaven, sweareth by the throne of God, and by him that sitteth thereon. Woe unto you, scribes and Pharisees, hypocrites! for ye pay tithe of mint and anise and cummin, and have omitted the weightier matters of the law, judgment, mercy, and faith: these ought ye to have done, and not to leave the other undone. Ye blind guides, which strain at a gnat, and swallow a camel".

In addition to representing wisdom, gold may also represent the Spirit, and it is believed that this is the meaning intended here. The scribes say that it is of no effect to swear by the temple (body), but that he that swears by the gold (Spirit) of the temple is held responsible. Christ tells us that the "temple" or body should also be holy because the Spirit dwelling in it and functioning through it should have a holy "house".

The altar represents the seat of the Life Force, that Force in which we live and move and have our being. The gift on the altar is the Force. There may be a difference among interpreters as to exactly what the altar is, however, since one "altar" (the brazen altar) is in the sacral region of the body and the other "altar" is in the head. The "gift" or Force plays through both of these "altars". Christ tells us that the physical seat of this Force (the generative region of the body) should be as holy as the Force that manifests through it, for the Force should sanctify the expression through which it flows.

The sentence, "For ye pay tithe of mint, and anise, and cummin", means that the scribes and Pharisees keep those laws which do not inconvenience them, but do not keep the laws which cause them any hardship. This is on the order of the religion of the masses today; they do that which does not inconvenience them, but the living of a pure life, which requires effort is not considered necessary by them.

"Woe unto you, scribes and Pharisees, hypocrites! for ye make clean the outside of the cup and of the platter, but within they are full of extortion and excess. Thou blind Pharisees, cleanse first that which is within the cup and platter, that the outside of them may be clean also. Woe anto you, scribes and Pharises, hypcrites! for ye are like anto whited sepulchres, which indeed appear beautiful outward, but are within full of dead men's bones, and of all ancleanness. Even so ye also outwardly appear righteous unto men, but within ye are full of hypocrisy and iniquity".

The "cup" spoken of in these verses is the "sacrament cup" in the sacral region of the body. This is the receptacle of the Life Force. The "platter" represents the body itself, which holds this "cup". There are many who make the outside of the body attractive but who lead lives of such low emotions that their inner selves are quite unclean. The "whited sepulchre" is an apt illustration of this. To the merely physical sight these people are clean, but to the spiritual sight they are not.

The story of the whited sepulchre gives us another hint. Those who possess only physical sight see merely its outside. Those with spiritual sight see the disintegration of the chemical and life ethers, besides the disintegration of the physical body, which is a very gruesome sight. The occult student knows that the body should be cremated after three and a half days, during which time the Spirit transfers the life experience. Cremation prevents the slow decay of the ethers and does not cause the person to be magnetized or attracted by the body, as it does to some extent when the body is not cremated. Cremation also prevents the noisome sight to spiritual eyes of the decaying ethers hovering over the dead bodies of persons who have passed on.

"Woe unto you, scribes and Pharisees, hypocrites! because ye build the tombs of the prophets, and garnish the sepulchres of the righteous. And say, If we had been in the days of our fathers, we would not have been partakers with them in the blood of the prophets. Wherefore ye be witnesses unto yourselves, that ye are the children of them which killed the prophets. Fill ye up then the measure of your fathers. Ye serpents, ye generation of vipers, how can ye escape the damnation of hell? Wherefore, behold, I send unto you prophets, and wise men, and scribes: and some of them ye shall kill and crucify; and some of them shall ye scourge in your synagogues, and persecute them from city to city: That upon you may come all the righteous blood shed upon the earth, from the blood of righteous

Abel unto the blood of Zacharias son of Barachias, whom ye slew between the temple and the altar. Verily I say unto you, All these things shall come upon this generation. O Jerusalem, Jerusalem, thou that killest the prophets, and stonest them which are sent unto thee, how often would I have gathered thy children together, even as a hen gathereth her chickens under her wings, and ye would not! Behold, your house is left unto you desolate. For I say unto you, Ye shall not see me henceforth, till ye shall say, Blessed is he that cometh in the name of the Lord".

The hypocrisy of observing merely the outward form of religion and not living the spiritual side of it is brought forcibly to our attention. To "build the tombs of the prophets" symbolizes the building of churches or institutions of worship where the spirit of religion is absent. Jerusalem, the "dome of the temple", represents the mental phase of the being in the above verses. Christ, the love principle, wishes to take the mental side under His wing and warm it with His love. The mind, however, rejects Him at this time, as it is not yet ready. It will not see Him again until it has evolved to the point that it is ready to receive Him gratefully. This is the condition of humanity today. It will only be when the mind has advanced far enough so that it is ready to welcome the Christ teachings that we can receive the permanent spiritual benefits thereof.

CHAPTER 24.

"And Jesus went out, and departed from the temple: and his disciples came to him for to shew him the buildings of the temple. And Jesus said unto them, See ye not all these things? verily I say unto you, There shall not be left here one stone upon another, that shall not be thrown down. And as he sat upon the mount of Olives, the disciples came unto him privately, saying, Tell us, when shall these things be? and what shall be the sign of thy coming, and of the end of the world? And Jesus answered and said unto them, Take heed that no man deceive you. For many shall come in my name, saying, I am Christ; and shall deceive many".

Christ leaving the temple symbolizes the Spirit leaving the body in its higher vehicles, In the literal story Christ leaves His body. The Disciples wish information. He tells them that "There shall not be left one stone upon another", meaning that the atoms of the body ("stones") will in time return to their original state. This is the natural process when the Spirit leaves the body at death. The atoms of the physical body are separated, and also the atoms of the lower ethers, which disintegrate with the physical body.

Later, the higher ethers of the vital body and the desire body are also disintegrated when the Spirit passes on to finer realms.

The mount of Olives is the "mount of peace" and signifies a lofty spiritual plane. The Disciples come to Christ on this plane and are taught certain truths, among them the coming of the end of the world, which happens both Cosmically and individually. Christ said that many shall profess to be the Christ and will deceive many. In one sense this means that when we become psychic many spirits and entities will attempt to deceive us by pretending to be the Christ or some other great teacher. Thousands of people are fooled in this way every day by psychics, who are themselves deceived by spirits posing as Christ, St. Germaine and many others.

"And ye shall hear of wars and rumors of wars: see that ye be not troubled: for all these things must come to pass, but the end is not yet. For nation shall rise against nation, and kingdom against kingdom: and there shall be famines, and pestilences, and earthquakes, in divers places. All these are the beginning of sorrows".

In the personal application, the "end of the world" is the end of materiality. The coming of Christ is the coming of the Christ Consciousness to each of us. We are told what is to happen when we go through the process necessary to become "Master Masons" or real disciples of Christ. The "wars" shall be the wars of the lower nature against the higher, when the higher nature seeks to gain control. We are not to be troubled about these "wars" because they are necessary until the Beast Within is finally conquered. This is one of the first steps. That is why Christ says it shall not be the end, since it is only the first step.

"Nation rising against nation" is the war of the opposing faculties within. It must continue until the higher qualities conquer. "Kingdom against kingdom" expresses practically the came idea. "Famines" refer to a lack of spirituality or any other lack of consciousness that must be attained. "Pestilences" refer to the effects of the misuse of any part of the being, which results in this retribution or pestilence. "Earthquakes" symbolize the shaking that preceeds the opening or spinning of the spiritual vortices of the body, which must take place before release from the body is accomplished. The "beginning of sorrows" is the time when the Spirit groans for release from the physical body.

"Then shall they deliver you up to be afflicted, and shall kill you: and ye shall be hated of all nations for my name's sake. And then shall many be offended, and shall betray one another, and shall hate one another. And many false prophets shall rise, and shall deceive many. And because iniquity shall abound, the love of many shall wax cold. But he that shall endure unto the end, the same shall be saved".

It is like an affliction, this process of purification. The "nations" within us or faculties which are destructive will hate the newly growing spiritual qualities and will "fight" them. The many that are "offended" are those many ordinary qualities which are "offended" by the Christ Within, just as the multitude were offended with the Christ before His crucifixion. The lower nature, which is the "Judas" shall seek to betray the Christ Within. The many false prophets are those evil qualities which might be said to make disheartening "predictions" when we attain to the higher life, or which seek to discourage this work of the higher nature. For one example, the materialistic mind says that certain organs will degenerate if they are not used sensually, in order to discourage us from following the spiritual life.

Because iniquity shall abound, many shall "wax cold" and become discouraged and give up. But he "that shall endure unto the end" of the time necessary to accomplish the spiritualization process, shall be saved the necessity of suffering in Purgatory.

"And this gospel of the kingdom shall be preached in all the world for a witness unto all nations; and then shall the end come. When ye therefore shall see the abomination of desolation, spoken of by Daniel the prophet, stand in the holy place, (whoso readeth, let him understand:) Then let them which be in Judæa flee into the mountains: Let him which is on the housetop not come down to take anything out of his house: Neither let him which is in the field return back to take his clothes".

Esoterically, the first verse means that the influence of the Christ Force shall be felt throughout the entire body, and when complete purification shall have been attained to, this shall be the "end". The "abomination of desolation" is the misuse of the Life Force or the sinful "drinking" of the "wine" of the "communion cup" within the body. This "taketh away the daily sacrifice", since that daily sacrifice is that which is made of the lower man for God and the higher self.

When this "abomination" stands in the "holy place" or that part of the body which *should* be holy, it is time to "flee to the mountain" or to raise the consciousness. If we do not do this, we shall be destroyed by the lower self. Those who are "on the housetop" are those who dwell in a spiritual consciousness and who must not let their minds be lowered into materiality. The people living in Judæa represent those who follow the teaching of Christ. They are advised to "flee to the mountains" or raise themselves to a purer consciousness in order to starve out the lower self. This causes it to die for lack of "food". The man in the "field" is the man who is working to gain experience, especially along material lines. He is advised not to "return back to take his clothes". Clothes signify the outer or material phase of life. The man in the field is therefore warned to think of spiritual and not material things.

"And woe unto them that are with child, and to them that give suck in those days! But pray ye that your flight be not in the winter, neither on the sabbath day: For then shall be great tribulation, such as was not since the beginning of the world to this time, no, nor ever shall be. And except those days should be shortened, there should no flesh be saved: but for the elect's sake those days shall be shortened. Then if any man shall say unto you, Lo, here is Christ, or there; believe it not. For there shall arise false Christs, and false prophets, and shall shew great signs and wonders; insomuch that, if it were possible, they shall deceive the very elect. Behold, I have told you before. Wherefore if they shall say unto you, Behold, he is in the desert; go not forth: behold, he is in the secret chambers; believe it not. For as the lightning cometh out of the east, and shineth even unto the west; so shall also the coming of the Son of man be. For wheresoever the carcase is, there will the eagles be gathered together. Immediately after the tribulation of those days shall the sun be darkened, and the moon shall not give her light, and the stars shall fall from heaven, and the powers of the heavens shall be shaken: And then shall appear the sign of the Son of man in heaven: and then shall all the tribes of the earth mourn, and they shall see the Son of man coming in the clouds of heaven with power and great glory. And he shall send his angels with a great sound of a trumpet, and they shall gather together his elect from the four winds, from one end of heaven to the other. Now learn a parable of the fig tree; When his branch is yet tender, and putteth forth leaves, ye know that summer is nigh; So likewise ye, when ye shall see all these things, know that it is near, even at the doors. Verily I say unto you, This generation shall not pass, till all these things be fulfilled".

Those who are "with child" are those who are about to give birth to the Christ Child within, which is the result of the union or marriage of the spiritualized head and heart. It is very undesirable for such a person to be tempted by the lower nature at this time, as it might interfere with the successful completion of this "birth". Still later, after the birth has taken place and the "Christ Child" is being raised to "manhood", it is undesirable that the Life Force be used by the lower nature. This is the meaning of the phrase, "And to them that give suck in those days".

The "flight in winter" refers to the flight in old age. It is deplorable if we still have to combat the lower nature when old age is upon us. We will be almost incurable if the old unworthy emotions and thoughts have not become dead within us by this time.

The Sun is the ruler of Sunday or the Sabbath. This represents that time when the Life Force (which is ruled by the Sun) is strongest. This is not a good time to allow the lower nature to have sway, since the temptations will be much greater because of the added strength of the Force.

All of the above conditions cause grat suffering in the war between the lower and the higher selves. God does indeed "shorten" these days, in that the lower man loses his influence more and more as the Spirit grows stronger and stronger.

Many false teachers will appear to the neophyte. These teachers will fool the most careful. The comparison of the coming of the Son of Man to the lightning which comes from the east to the west describes that fire force which comes from the "east" or lower region of the body to the "west" or higher region. This is the path of the Christ Within. The reader will remember that the Tabernacle in the Wilderness extended from east to west, and that it is representative of the human body, the west room being the head.

Where the "carcass" is or where the Life Force is in the body, there also will be found the "eagles" or those phases of being which seek to devour this Force.

The Sun represents the mind and the Moon, the intuition or heart. The condition in which the Sun is darkened represents the perplexity of the mind which does not yet see the light, just before attainment. The Moon also being darkened shows that even the imagination will be without a clue as to what is to follow and will be "fearful".

The falling of the stars from heaven represents the fact that the seven centers of the desire body and the centers of the vital body become active in the neophyte. They are described as having "fallen from heaven" because they appear as spiritual forces in man, as the stars are spiritual forces in the heavens. The powers of the heavens that are "shaken" symbolizes the shaking sensation of these centers or "stars" preparatory to their spinning, which accomplishes the liberation of the Spirit from the body at the time of spiritual attainment. (Please read "Revelation, Esoterically Interpreted" by the author, in which the same conditions are described by St. John and interpreted by the author).

The sign of the Son of Man in the heavens may symbolize that light which begins to shine around the head of the individual who attains to illumination. The sound of the trumpet of the angels is the vibration which is created at this time. We know that vibration has its appropriate color and sound. The gathering together of the elect is the gathering together of the "elect" within us, the spiritual parts of us which are "gathered together" or concentrated at the time of attainment.

A fig tree is the symbol of productiveness. Therefore, Christ tells us that when spiritual productiveness begins to manifest in the occult student, he may know that attainment is at hand or at the very "door". A door is an opening or entrance and this is a sign that enlightenment will flow through the "doors" into the consciousness of the aspirant.

As proof that Christ was referring to spiritual conditions and processes within the individual and not merely to literal happenings, we have it in His words that, "This generation shall not pass till all these things be fulfilled". We know that these things did not happen in a literal sense, since the falling of the stars from heaven to earth would have destroyed the earth. Some of those who were receiving Christ's teachings went through the processes described, hence Christ stated that some of them would not die until these things were fulfilled.

"Heaven and earth shall pass away, but my words shall not pass away. But of that day and hour knoweth no man, no, not the angels of heaven, but my Father only. But as the days of Noe were, so shall also the coming of the Son of man be. For as in the days that were before the flood they were eating and drinking, marrying and giving in marriage, until the day that Noe entered into the Ark, And knew not until the flood came, and took them all away; so shall also the coming of the Son of man be. Then shall two be in the field; the one shall be taken, and the other left. Two women shall be grinding at the mill; the one shall be taken, and the other left".

The statement, "Heaven and earth shall pass away", may be interpreted both individually and Cosmically. In our evolution we know that there are great Cosmic nights in which even the planets are re-absorbed in God for a period of rest. They are brought forth again for the next day of manifestation. (See "Cosmo Conception"). From the individual viewpoint, the old heaven and earth symbolize the old viewpoint or conception of both spiritual and physical things. We acquire a new spiritual consciousness or "heaven" and a new body or "earth" that has become purified. No one knows either the time of the Cosmic "night" or the time when the old consciousness of the individual will be renewed.

Noe or Noah represents the Initiate who has built the soul body or "ark" which is able to rise above the "waters" of generation. These lower emotions destroy those of humanity who have not built the "ark". This ark historically symbolizes the new type body built by the pioneers of Atlantis, who were able to climb 'to the highlands and breathe the new atmosphere that came when the basins of Atlantis were flooded. The masses who had not built this "ark" or new type body were drowned.

When the Christ comes, the people of the world will be engaged in everyday tasks, but those who have built the soul body or "golden wedding garment" will be caught up in the air to meet Him. Those who have not, will be left in spiritual darkness.

"Watch therefore: for ye know not what hour your Lord doth come. But know this, that if the goodman of the house had known in what watch the thief would come, he would have watched, and would not have suffered his house to be broken up. Therefore be ye also ready: for in such an hour as ye think not the Son of man cometh. Who then is a faithful and wise servant, whom his lord hath made ruler over his household, to give them meat in due season? Blessed is that servant, whom his lord when he cometh shall find so doing. Verily I say unto you, That he shall make him ruler over all his goods. But and if that evil servant shall say in his heart, My lord delayeth his coming; And shall begin to smite his fellowservants, and to eat and drink with the drunken; The lord of that servant shall come in a day when he looketh not for him, and in an hour that he is not aware of, And shall cut him asunder, and appoint him his portion with the hypocrites: there shall be weeping and gnashing of teeth".

We are told that eternal vigilance is the price of safety and that it is not enough for us to occasionally raise the level of our consciousness. We must fight the good fight to the end and maintain this consciousness continually, or the lower nature (the "thief") will try to come back. It is the belief of the writer that even an Initiate may lose out after he has attained. That is, he may lose the ability and privilege of meeting with the Brothers in the Temple and assisting them in their great humanitarian work, if he does not maintain the high rate of vibration necessary.

CHAPTER 25.

"Then shall the kingdom of heaven be likened unto ten virgins, which took their lamps, and went forth to meet the bridegroom. And five of them were wise, and five were foolish. They that were foolish took their lamps, and took no oil with them: But the wise took oil in their vessels with their lamps. While the bridegroom tarried, they all slumbered and slept. And at midnight there was a cry made, Behold, the bridegroom cometh; go ye out to meet him. Then all those virgins arose, and trimmed their lamps. And the foolish said unto the wise, Give us of your oil: for our lamps are gone out. But the wise answered, saying, Not so; lest there be not enough for us and you: but go ye rather to them that sell, and buy for yourselves. And when they went to buy, the bridegroom came; and they that were ready went in with him to the marriage: and the door was shut. Afterward came also the other virgins, saying, Lord, Lord, open to us. But he answered and said, Verily I say unto you, I know you not. Watch therefore, for ye know neither the day nor the hour wherein the Son of man cometh".

The story of the ten virgins is one of the most important in the Bible from the esoteric viewpoint. The ten virgins represent the positive and negative poles of the five physical senses through which we contact the physical world. Ten also represents generation, since "1" is the positive or masculine pole and "0" the negative, feminine pole. The parable tells of those phases of the physical senses which waste the Life Force and of the senses which conserve the "Oil of Life".

(For a scientific explanation of the story of the virgins and the oil, read page 20 of "Revelation, Esoterically Interpreted" by the writer).

The "oil" in this story is an actual oil which is secreted in the cardia, the home of the Kundalini Fire. Five of the "virgins" retained and conserved this "oil" by living a regenerate life, and as a result lighted the "lamp" of their beings with a spiritual light that enabled them to meet the Christ ("bridegroom") and become "wedded" to Him. But the foolish virgins wasted this "oil" (through sensuality) until there was none left, and they were in spiritual darkness and could not respond to the Christ influence.

This parable has both a Cosmic and a personal meaning. No one who wastes the Life Force may attain to Initiation and the Christ Consciousness. In order to do this, we have to accumulate sufficient of this "Oil of Life". Only those who conserve this "oil" can be real Christians, for the Christian has to pass certain tests, among which are healing the sick and the ability to withstand the bites of poisonous snakes. It is the presence of this "oil" in the blood which counteracts the poison of the snake and also assists in the healing process when the Christian heals others. We are again reminded of the sanctity of the creative force and the necessity of conserving it, if we are to keep up with the pioneers of humanity and not become laggards in Life's School. Do not let the five "virgins" within yourself waste your precious "Oil of Life".

"For the kingdom of heaven is as a man travelling into a far country, who called his own servants, and delivered unto them his goods. And unto one he gave five talents, to another two, and to another one; to every man according to his several ability; and straightway took his journey. Then he that had received the five talents went and traded with the same, and made them other five talents. And likewise he that had received two, he also gained other two. But he that had received one went and digged in the earth, and hid his lord's money. After a long time the lord of those servants cometh, and reckoneth with them. And so he that had received five talents came and brought other five talents, saying, Lord, thou deliveredst unto me five talents: behold, I have gained beside them five talents more. His lord said unto him, Well done, thou good and faithful servant: thou hast been faithful over a few things, I will make thee ruler over many things: enter thou into the joy of thy lord. He also that had received two talents came and said, Lord, thou deliveredst unto me two talents: behold, I have gained two other talents beside them. His lord said unto him, Well done good and faithful servant; thou hast been faithful over a few things, I will make thee ruler over many things: enter thou into the joy of thy lord. Then he which had received the one talent came and said, Lord I knew thee that thou art an hard man, reaping where thou hast not sown, and gathering where thou hast not strawed: And I was afraid, and went and hid thy talent in the earth: lo, there thou hast that which is thine. His lord answered and said unto him, Thou wicked and slothful servant, thou knowest that I reap where I sowed not, and gather where I have not strawed: Thou oughtest therefore to have put my money to the exchangers, and then at my coming I should have received mine own with usury. Take therefore the talent from him, and give it unto him which hath ten talents. For unto every one that hath shall be given, and he shall have abundance: but from him that hath not shall be taken away even that which he hath. And cast ye the unprofitable servant into outer darkness: there shall be weeping and gnashing of teeth".

The man who travels to the far country represents God. The time is that time in the early evolution of man when the Bible says that God rested. This was the "seventh day" or that time when God withdrew from active guidance of infant mankind and allowed it to use its own free will to carve out its destiny. It also became responsible for its own acts. Mankind began to descend gradually into denser matter and to go farther away from the heaven worlds and the Father in consciousness. Actually, therefore, it was mankind that "travelled into a far country", though in the present story God is the one who goes away. The effect is just the same and therefore does not change the meaning or interpretation.

The talents that the man gave to his servants represent faculties which are capable of development. Mankind was given these faculties in a crude state in the beginning of his evolution. The servant who receives the five talents symbolizes an active individual belonging to the pioneer class. He doubles his faculties through intelligent activity. The servant who receives two talents is not as active as the first, but he also manages to increase that which he started with. The servant with the one talent is the individual who spends his time along earthy lines. He "buries" his talent in the "ground" or uses his faculties in a lower way. In one sense, the three servants may represent three great life waves, the human, animal and plant waves. In another sense, the five talents may be the five senses. We know that with spiritual development our senses will more than double in keenness and power. However, the individual who does not develop his senses will have them become dull, so that he will finally "lose" them. This parable is also a hint that we should not waste our opportunities. As Omar Khayyam expresses it.

"The wine of life keeps oozing drop by drop,
The leaves of life keep falling, one by one".

(Students of the spiritual might be interested in reading an esoteric interpretation of selected verses from this poem. It is in the booklet, "Occult Interpretations" by the writer).

"When the Son of man shall come in his glory, and all the holy angels with him, then shall he sit upon the throne of his glory: And before him shall be gathered all nations and he shall separate them one from another, as a shepherd divideth his sheep from the goats: And he shall set the sheep on his right hand, but the goats on the left. Then shall the King say unto them on his right hand, Come, ye blessed of my Father, inherit the kingdom prepared for you from the foundation of the world: For I was an hungered, and ye gave me meat: I was thirsty, and ye gave me drink: I was a stranger, and ye took me in: Naked, and ye clothed me: I was sick, and ye visited me: I was in prison, and ye came unto me. Then shall the righteous answer him saying, Lord, when saw we thee an hungered, and fed thee? or thirsty, and gave thee drink? When saw we thee a stranger, and took thee in? or naked, and clothed thee? Or when saw we thee sick, or in prison, and came unto thee? And the King shall answer and say unto them, Verily I say unto you. Inasmuch as ye have done it unto one of the least of these my brethren, ye have done it unto me. Then shall he say also unto them on the left hand, Depart from me, ye cursed, into everlasting fire, prepared for the devil and his angels: For I was an hungered, and ye gave me no meat: I was thirsty, and ye gave me no drink: I was a stranger and ye took me not in: naked, and ye clothed me not: sick and in prison, and ye visited me not. Then shall they also answer him, saying, Lord, when saw we thee an hungered, or athirst, or a stranger, or naked, or sick, or in prison, and did not minister unto thee? Then shall he answer them, saying, Verily I say uto you, Inasmuch as ye did it not to one of the least of these, ye did it not to me. And these shall go away into everlasting punishment: but the righteous into life eternal".

This hunger of the Christ refers to the hungering of the Christ Within for a purer body in which to function and a purer mind with which to think, and other improved faculties, so that His suffering in the physical body will not be so great. His being thirsty refers to his "thirst" for the raised "water of life", which brings spiritual illumination and purifies the body. The body is usually made "a den of thieves" which "steals" away the higher attributes. This Christ Within is a "stranger" until we take Him in and let Him "sup" with us. He is "naked" or without the spiritual vehicles developed so that He can function consciously, and at the same time, He is without power because we do not cultivate the spiritual life which allows Him to show forth this power. He is "sick and in "prison" because the Spirit is weak and ill through being confined in a body or "prison" which is impure.

Those of us who realize the condition we are in and who begin to make of ourselves fit places for the Christ Spirit to dwell are those who do all of the kind things which the Christ says are done by those who sit "on the right hand". It also means that those who minister unto others are at the same time ministering to the "Christ" within those brethren whom they help.

Those who live a sensual, material life are those who refuse to assist the Christ Within themselves and others, who is sick, hungry, thirsty and naked, because of the condition of the body and mind and heart. They are those who will not be able to receive the Cosmic Christ when He comes again because they will not have built any of the higher qualities by which they would be able to meet Him. St. Paul says that we shall be "caught up in the air to meet Him", and this process will require a much greater state of spiritual development than we possess at the present time.

CHAPTER 26.

"And it came to pass, when Jesus had finished all these sayings, he said unto his disciples, Ye know that after two days is the feast of the passover and the Son of man is betrayed to be crucified. Then assembled together the chief priests, and the scribes, and the elders of the people, unto the palace of the high priest, who was called Caiaphas, And consulted that they might take Jesus by subtilty, and kill him, But they said, Not on the feast day, lest there be an uproar among the people".

This "feast of the passover" celebrates the passing over of the children of Israel or "children of light" from a condition of spiritual darkness, symbolized by Egypt, to the greater understanding and illumination that comes to them when they go into the "Promised land", after having wandered in the "desert" or gone through a period of preparation. Each of us in time will celebrate the "feast of the passover" within ourselves.

The chief priests and the scribes represent those phases of the mind which would destroy the Spirit by binding it tightly with a religion of form. St. Paul tells us that, "The letter killeth the spirit". The people represent the common consciousness, and the destructive phases of the mind are afraid that this ordinary consciousness will rebel at their methods if they do not work craftily.

"Now when Jesus was in Bethany, in the house of Simon the leper. There came unto him a woman having an alabaster box of very precious ointment, and poured it on his head, as he sat at meat. But when his disciples saw it, they had indignation, saying, To what purpose is this waste? For this ointment might have been sold for much, and given to the poor. When Jesus understood it, he said unto them, Why trouble ye the woman? for she hath wrought a good work upon me. For ye have the poor always with you; but me ye have not always. For in that she hath poured this ointment on my body, she did it for my burial. Verily I say unto you, Wheresoever this gospel shall be preached in the whole world, there shall also this, that this woman hath done, be told for a memorial of her".

Simon, the leper, represents a part of the being which is yet unclean, and the Christ being in his "house" signifies that a process of cleansing and spiritualization is going on in this part of the body. Christ gives us this story as a symbol of what we ourselves must do. The woman symbolizes the repentant and spiritualized emotional nature, the ointment, the Life Force, and the alabaster box, the seat of this Force. Pouring the ointment upon the head of Christ is the raising of this Life Force to the head through the aid of the pure emotional nature, which results in illumination.

The meaning of the last verse is that this same process must eventually take place within all of humanity. The Life Force is symbolized by the precious ointment because the purification and upliftment of this Force is a very "sweet" and fragrant experience in an occult sense.

In some of the other Gospels, it is told of the woman washing the feet of Jesus. This is a somewhat similar process because the Life Force is alo conducted to the feet. When these processes are gone through, three extra pairs of spinal nerves are brought to life and the person becomes attuned to the solar month instead of the lunar month. Then many new things are in store for him, both spiritually and physically.

"Then one of the twelve, called Judas Iscariot, went unto the chief priests, And said unto them, What will ye give me, and I will deliver him unto you? And they covenanted with him for thirty pieces of silver. And from that time he sought opportunity to betray him."

Judas Iscariot represents the lower nature, the sensual phase of being, which is constantly seeking to betray and "crucify" the Christ Within. The priests and scribes represent phases of the mind through which this "Judas" can work, in order to bring about his ends. Silver represents the Moon forces, which we know play such a part in the liquids of the body and in generation. It is possible to go into detail concerning the physiological working of this part of the story, but it is thought best for the neophyte to meditate upon this for himself. The more advanced student, of course, understands it thoroughly already.

"Now the first day of the feast of unleavened bread the disciples came to Jesus, saying unto him, Where wilt thou that we prepare for thee to eat the passover? And he said, Go into the city to such a man, and say unto him, the Master saith, My time is at hand; I will keep the passover at thy house with my disciples. And the disciples did as Jesus had appointed them; and they made ready the passover. Now when the even was come, he sat down with the twelve. And as they did eat, he said, Verily I say unto you, that one of you shall betray me. And they were exceeding sorrowful, and began every one of them to say unto him, Lord, is it I? And he answered and said, He that dippeth his hand with me in the dish, the same shall betray me. The Son of man goeth as it is written of him: but woe unto that man by whom the Son of man is betrayed! it had been good for that man if he had not been born. Then Judas, which betrayed him, answered and said, Master, is it I? He said unto him, Thou hast said".

The passover represents the "passing over" or transition from one state of consciousness to another higher one. The man in whose house the passover is to be kept is described in other Gospels as a man bearing a pitcher of water on his shoulder. This is the symbol of the Aquarian Age when all humanity shall "pass over" to a more Christ-like state of consciousness. Individually, it means that each of us must raise our consciousness to a newer, higher one before we can have "supper" with the Christ. Christ tells us plainly that the supper of the passover takes place in the head (an upper chamber). The Aquarian Man with the balanced urn upon his shoulder portrays the future man who will have perfect control of the "Water of Life".

The one who dipped with the Christ in the dish represents that part of us that attempts to misuse the "Wine of Life" which is in the "sacrament cup" of the body or the "dish". In other words, it is the lower nature or the "Judas Iscariot" within each of us, which seeks to use the Life Force in sensual living. It is the traitor which betrays us continually until we have followed, in our own lives, each step in the life of Christ, until this "Judas" has "hanged" himself and has no more influence over us.

"And as they were eating, Jesus took bread, and blessed it, and brake it, and gave it to the disciples, and said, Take, eat; this is my body. And he took the cup, and gave thanks, and gave it to them, saying, Drink ye all of it: For this is my blood of the new testament, which is shed for many, for the remission of sins. But I say unto you, I will not drink henceforth of this fruit of the vine, until that day when I drink it new with you in my Father's kingdom".

It is not generally known that it is because the great Christ Spirit enters into the aura of our earth each year, that the grain is fructified and the seeds germinated and all life is renewed. Each morsel of food that we take into our bodies is made possible by this yearly "sacrifice" of the Christ. In a sense, we are partaking of His "body" or life in each particle of food that we eat.

The "wine" which fills the "sacrament cup" is, of course, the Life Force. It is of the "new testament" or new prophecy since the coming of Christ. The new prophecy is concerning its use. We must "drink" or absorb all of it and not use any part of it in sensuality, if we desire to attain divine illumination. Christ says that He will not partake of this Force any longer in the physical world as a man, but will partake of it closer to its source, in the "Father's house", in a newer or purer state.

"And when they had sung an hymn, they went out into the mount of Olives. Then saith Jesus unto them, All ye shall be offended because of me this night: for it is written, I will smite the shepherd, and the sheep of the flock shall be scattered abroad. But after I am risen again, I will go before you into Galilee. Peter answered and said unto him, Though all men shall be offended because of thee, yet will I never be offended. Jesus said unto him, Verily I say unto thee, That this night, before the cock crow, thou shalt deny me thrice. Peter said unto him, Though I should die with thee, yet will I not deny thee. Likewise also said all the disciples".

Many of us go to the "mount of Olives" after we have sung a "hymn". This means that after raising ourselves nearer to God through devotional service, our consciousness ascends to the higher realms, where PEACE prevails. We think that when we attain to this condition and are thrilled to the divine power and light which flows through us that we will never again stoop to low things and deny the Christ Within. We soon find, however, that we are to play the part of Peter many times before we finally attain to our own "crucifixion" and liberation from the cross of the body.

"Then cometh Jesus with them unto a place called Gethsemane, and saith unto the disciples, Sit ye here, while I go and pray yonder. And he took with him Peter and the two sons of Zebedee, and began to be sorrowful and very heavy. Then saith he unto them, My soul is exceeding sorrowful even unto death: tarry ye here, and watch with me. And he went a little farther, and fell on his face, and prayed, saying, O my Father, if it be possible, let this cup pass from me: nevertheless not as I will, but as thou wilt. And he cometh unto the disciples, and findeth them asleep, and saith unto Peter, What, could ye not watch with me one hour? Watch and pray, that ye enter not into temptation: the spirit indeed is willing, but the flesh is weak. He went away again the second time, and prayed, saying, O my Father, if this cup may not pass away from me, except I drink it, thy will be done. And he came and found them asleep again: for their eyes were heavy. And he left them, and went away again, and prayed the third time, saying the same words. Then cometh he to his disciples, and saith unto them, Sleep on now, and take your rest: behold, the hour is at hand, and the Son of man is betrayed into the hands of sinners. Rise, let us be going: behold, he is at hand that doth betray me".

Gethsemane means "wisdom through sorrow", and each of us must go through the experiences by which we attain wisdom. When we become more advanced than the masses we must experience much sorrow caused by the loneliness that comes to us when friends and loved ones fail and forsake us, and even our very own faculties betray us.

Christ endeavors, in the Garden, to take His three most highly developed Disciples to a greater plane of consciousness, but it is impossible at the time. The Bible says that they "fell asleep", which indicates that they could not be awakened to the higher consciousness that the Christ wished.

This experience in the Garden of Gethsemane and the betrayal must be lived to be understood, for it is an inner experience. The fact that Christ prayed three times shows us that it is not always possible to be able immediately to make our wills subservient to the will of God, but we must make the effort several times. We must also be content to stand absolutely alone and without help and allow the God Within to have its way.

"And while he yet spake, lo, Judas, one of the twelve, came, and with him a great multitude with swords and staves, from the chief priests and elders of the people. Now he that betrayed him gave them a sign, saying, Whomsoever I shall kiss, that same is he: hold him fast. And forthwith he came to Jesus, and said, Hail, master; and kissed him. And Jesus said unto him, Friend, wherefore art thou come? Then came they, and laid hands on Jesus, and took him. And, behold, one of them which were with Jesus stretched out his hand, and drew his sword and struck a servant of the high priest's, and smote off his ear. Then said Jesus unto him, Put up again thy sword into his place: for all they that take the sword shall perish with the sword. Thinkest thou that I cannot now pray to my Father, and he shall presently give me more than twelve legions of angels? But how then shall the scriptures be fulfilled, that thus it must be?"

The lesson in these verses is that the lower nature, Judas, always betrays the Christ Within in a subtle manner, symbolized by the kiss. The methods of the lower nature are those which entice the senses. He endeavors to turn over the power of the body to the material being or the "multitude".

We learn in the instance of the striking off the servant's ear that we cannot attain to Initiation or illumination through fighting sin. Fighting it only gives it more strength. When we fight a thing, we also have to descend to its level. Indifference is the only successful means with which to fight evil and conquer the animal nature.

"Who lives by the sword must die by the sword" is a world famous quotation. This is another illustration of the law of Cause and Effect or the Mosaic Law. These verses warn us not to try to gain spirituality through severe, forced methods, but only through the Love-Wisdom path of the Christ.

"In that same hour said Jesus to the multitudes, Are ye come out as against a thief with swords and staves for to take me? I sat daily with you teaching in the temple, and ye laid no hold on me. But all this was done, that the scriptures of the prophets might be fulfilled. Then all the disciples forsook him and fled. And they that had laid hold on Jesus led him away to Caiaphas the high priest, where the scribes and the elders were assembled. But Peter followed him afar off unto the high priest's palace, and went in, and sat with the servants, to see the end".

"Staves" and "swords" both symbolize the avenue of the Life Force, which is the spinal cord. This Force may be used for either good or evil. It may be conserved and raised up the spinal cord, or it may descend in the opposite direction in sensuality. We will remember that an angel guarded the gates of the "Garden of Eden" with a flaming sword. This "sword" or "staff" or spinal cord may either open the way to the higher consciousness or it may bar it, depending upon the way we use our Life Force.

The fleeing of the Disciples describes a common occurrence, when the Spirit is betrayed by the lower nature and the spiritual faculties no longer aid it.

"Now the chief priests, and elders, and all the council, sought false witness against Jesus, to put him to death; But found none: yea, though many false witnesses came, yet found they none. At last came two false witnesses, And said, This fellow said, I am able to destroy the temple of God, and to build it in three days. And the high priest arose, and said unto him, Answereth thou nothing? what is it which these witness against thee? But Jesus held his peace. And the high priest answered and said unto him, I adjure thee by the living God, that thou tell us whether thou be the Christ, the Son of God. Jesus said unto him, Thou hast said: nevertheless I say unto you, Hereafter shall ye see the Son of man sitting on the right hand of power, and coming in the clouds of heaven".

It is possible that in these verses is hidden the same meaning as that symbolized by the Crucifixion of Jesus between the two thieves. The two thieves and the two witnesses would represent, in each case, the head and the heart before they had become spiritualized. When the head and the heart are not spiritualized, they will always testify against the Christ Within because they are not capable of understanding spiritual things and condemn what they do not understand. The chief priest is the purely intellectual mind which can only understand a religion of form or ritual. He cannot nor *does* not understand the Christ.

"Then the high priest rent his clothes, saying, He hath spoken blasphemy; what further need have we of witnesses? behold, now ye have heard his blasphemy. What think ye? They answered and said, He is guilty of death. Then did they spit on his face, and buffeted him; and others smote him with the palms of their hands. Saying, Prophesy unto us, thou Christ, Who is he that smote thee".

These verses are very significant. The abuses put to the Christ describe some of the different misuses of the Life Force. This will only be understood by deeper students. The writer does not believe it good taste to go into detail concerning these things. He can only suggest that the student consider his own life and then meditate on these verses for their hidden meaning.

"Now Peter sat without in the palace: and a damsel came unto him, saying, Thou also wast with Jesus of Galilee. But he denied before them all, saying, I know not what thou sayest. And when he was gone out into the porch, another maid saw him, and said unto them that were there, This fellow was also with Jesus of Nazereth. And again he denied with an oath, I do not know the man. And after a while came unto him they that stood by, and said to Peter, Surely thou also art one of them; for thy speech betrayeth thee. Then began he to curse and to swear, saying, I know not the man. And immediately the cock crew. And Peter remembered the word of Jesus, which said unto him, Before the cock crow, thou shalt deny me thrice. And he went out and wept bitterly".

Peter represents Faith. His denial of the Christ is the losing of our faith when we reach that point in our spiritual careers when we must pass the most severe of all tests and our faith in the Christ Within becomes weak. Intuition might be the first maid who questions Peter. This intuition reminds us that we once possessed this faith in the Christ Within. When we realize we have failed the test, we are exceedingly sorrowful. If we persevere, however, some day our faith will become strong. Then, even though we slip back into "Egypt", we will come out each time with more courage and faith until we finally conquer.

CHAPTER 27.

"When the morning was come, all the chief priests and elders of the people took counsel against Jesus to put him to death: And when they had bound him, they led him away, and delivered him to Pontius Pilate the governor. Then Judas, which had betrayed him, when he saw that he was condemned, repented himself, and brought again the thirty pieces of silver to the chief priests and elders. Saying, I have sinned in that I have betrayed innocent blood. And they said, What is that to us? see thou to that. And he cast down the pieces of silver in the temple, and departed, and went and hanged himself. And the chief priests took the silver pieces, and said, It is not lawful for to put them into the treasury, because it is the price of blood. And they took counsel, and bought with them the potter's field to bury strangers in. Wherefore that field was called, The field of blood unto this day. Then was fulfilled that which was spoken by Jeremy the prophet, saying, And they took the thirty pieces of silver, the price of him that was valued, whom they of the children of Israel did value; And gave them for the potter"s field, as the Lord appointed me".

This process of the betrayal of the Christ Within to the lower phases of being is one that we all experience many times on the occult path, until we no longer allow this drama to be re-enacted within ourselves. "Judas" always repents after the "betrayal", since it becomes evident that "the game is not worth the candle". The pieces of silver, which are "the price of the blood", indicate that this Force which is wasted as a result of sensuality takes the equivalent of so much blood from the body. However, since it is an occult rule not to dwell upon ugly things but to let the mind think as much as possible of the good, the true and the beautiful, we will touch but lightly upon this part of the story.

The potter's field also emphasizes the misuse of the Life Force (since it is the "burial place" of unknown and unwanted ones.) The "silver" or Moon force "buys" this "field" when the Life Force is used sensually and not for the purpose of generating physical bodies.

"And Jesus stood before the governor: and the governor asked him, saying, Art thou the King of the Jews? and Jesus said unto him, Thou sayest. And when he was accused of the chief priests and elders, he answered nothing. Then said Pilate unto him, Hearest thou not how many things they witness against thee? And he answered him to never a word; insomuch that the governor marvelled greatly".

The governor represents material power or the material mind, which does not speak the same language as the Christ Spirit. The Christ Within never answers to these lower parts of the being. It is only when we spiritualize ourselves that we can hear the soft voice of the Christ Within. This "Christ" does not defend itself or argue with the material nature, as represented by the various officials in the verses above.

"Now at that feast the governor was wont to release unto the people a prisoner, whom they would. And they had then a notable prisoner, called Barabbas. Therefore when they were gathered together, Pilate said unto them, Whom will ye that I release unto you? Barabbas, or Jesus which is called Christ? For he knew that for envy they had delivered him. When he was set down on the judgment seat, his wife sent unto him, saying, Have thou nothing to do with that just man: for I have suffered many things this day in a dream because of him. But the chief priests and elders persuaded the multitude that they should ask Barabbas, and destroy Jesus. The governor answered and said unto them, Whether of the twain will ye that I release unto you? They said, Barabbas. Pilate saith unto them, What shall I do then with Jesus which is called Christ? They all say unto him, Let him be crucified. And the governor said, Why, what evil hath he done? But they cried out the more, saying, Let him be crucified. When Pilate saw that he could prevail nothing, but that rather a tumult was made, he took water, and washed his hands before the multitude, saying, I am innocent of the blood of this just person: see ye to it. Then answered all the people, and said, His blood be on us, and on our children. Then released he Barabbas unto them: and when he had scourged Jesus, he delivered him to be crucified'.

This feast at which it was the custom that the governor release a prisoner symbolizes that time within ourselves when the mind (Pilate) must decide between the clamorous senses and the higher self. In this case, the decision is being made along what might be called normal lines. That is, the senses have their way. The mind really wishes to choose the higher life, but the physical senses are too strong and the mind is not able to enforce its will against the clamoring of the lower desires. Pilate's wife symbolizes Intuition. She feels that the Christ Within must not be harmed and she warns the reasoning mind (Pilate) concerning this. The chief priests and the elders (purely mentally-religious phases of being) cannot understand the Christ Within and wish it destroyed. Here is much room for meditation. Form religion always destroys spirituality.

When the reasoning mind sees that it cannot contend with the common consciousness (the multitude), it is forced to yield to its wishes, even though it realizes it is wrong in doing so. Have not many of us gone throught the same experience, when our physical desires have caused us to yield to something which we knew in our minds to be wrong?

The meaning of the line, "His blood be on us and on our children", is that when we misuse the spiritual force, or spill the "blood" of the Christ Within, we must pay for it in impaired mental and physical well-being until we have completely overcome the ill effects. This may take many lives and many, many generations.

"Then the soldiers of the governor took Jesus into the common hall, and gathered unto him the whole band of soldiers. And they stripped him, and put on him a scarlet robe. And when they had platted a crown of thorns, they put it upon his head, and a reed in his right hand: and they bowed the knee before him, and mocked him, saying, Hail, King of the Jews! And they spit upon him, and took the reed, and smote him on the head. And after that they had mocked him, they took the robe off him, and put his own raiment on him, and led him away to crucify him".

This also describes the lower use of the Life Force, which as mentioned before, the writer will not explain in detail. Let him who has "eyes to see" and a heart capable of understanding meditate upon these verses carefully. Suffice to say that each character in the story symbolizes some faculty or phase of being or part of the body which enters into the generative act.

—It should be emphasized, however, that the time which elapses between the various abuses put to the Christ and the time of the Crucifixion is of somewhat different duration, depending upon what interpretation of the story is used. By different interpretations we mean the literal, the physiological, or the Cosmic, etc.

"And as they came out, they found a man of Cyrene, Simon by name: him they compelled to bear his cross".

Simon was said to be a dark man and symbolizes the same Life Force which was previously used by the neophyte in sensuality. After the degradation and suffering incident to the abuse of the Christ Force (which story we have just finished), the neophyte then turns the Life Force upward constructively, and it assists the Christ to carry the "cross".

"And when they were come unto a place called Golgotha, that is to say, a place of a skull, They gave him vinegar to drink mingled with gall: and when he had tasted thereof, he would not grink. And they crucified him, and parted his garments, casting lots: that it might be fulfilled which was spoken by the prophet, They parted my garments among them, and upon my vesture did they cast lots. And sitting down they watched him there: And set up over his head his accusation written, THIS IS JESUS THE KING OF THE JEWS.

The "place of the skull", Golgotha, is the parietal-occipital suture in the head from which the Spirit leaves the body at night during sleep and also at death. As an Initiate, the Ego also leaves the body consciously at this point in the head. The bitter drink which Christ refused to drink may symbolize the fact that when the person has attained to the consciousness necessary for this high step, there can be no bitterness in his heart. Such a person stands ready to forgive and send out only love to those who would persecute and "crucify" him.

The casting of lots for Christ's garments may indicate the separation of the vehicles which is necessary when the neophyte is ready for Initiation. We are taught that the separation of the desire body took place ages ago, but the separation of the vital body is one of the steps in Initiation. This "casting of lots" may mean that the lower ethers of the vital body are segregated for use by the purely physical nature, while the higher ethers or parts of the "garment" are used by the spiritual self. For example, the chemical and the life ethers of the vital body are used for assimilation, excretion and propagation, which are phases of material life. The light and reflecting ethers are used for sense perception, blood heat and memory which are higher activities of the Spirit.

The people "sitting down" to watch Christ upon the cross indicates that the ordinary consciousness (people) can take no further part in the process of leaving the body. This has to be left to the Spirit. The two thieves crucified with Christ are the unspiritualized heart and the unspiritualized mind. They are compared to thieves because they "steal" from the spiritual consciousness until they have become purified through suffering.

We are told that in reality there were more than two

people crucified at the same time as Christ. This appears to be one of the instances in which the actual happening is slightly changed by the writers of the Bible in order to bring out more forcibly a hidden truth. Note carefully that St. Matthew does not deny that there were more crucified at this time. He merely mentions the two thieves, which does not detract from the actual happening.

"And they that passed by reviled him, wagging their heads, And saying, Thou that destroyest the temple, and buildest it in three days, save thyself. If thou be the Son of God, come down from the cross. Likewise also the chief priests mocking him, with the scribes and elders, said, He saved others; himself he cannot save. If he be the King of Israel, let him now come down from the cross, and we will believe him. He trusted in God; let him deliver him now, if he will have him: for he said, I am the Son of God. The thieves also, which were crucified with him, cast the same in his teeth".

We must all, as aspirants toward liberation from the "cross" of the body, expect to be reviled and misunderstood. We must also expect the unspiritualized attributes of our own bodies to cry out against the activity of the Christ working in us. We will be taunted in an effort to tempt us to demonstrate our spiritual power and to prove spiritual truths. We will be asked to give a "sign" or to misuse spiritual power merely to satisfy the curiosity of those who are undeveloped spiritually. The lower traits within us will tempt us to use spiritual power for material ends. "He saved others; himself he cannot save" (or *will* not save) is the maxim of the Initiate, who will not use his divine power for self, but only for others.

"Now from the sixth hour there was darkness over all the land unto the ninth hour. And about the ninth hour Jesus cried with a loud voice, saying, Eli, Eli, lama sabachthani? that is to say, My God, my God, why hast thou forsaken me? Some of them that stood there, when they heard that said, This man calleth for Elias. And straightway one of them ran, and took a sponge, and filled it with vinegar, and put it on a reed, and gave him to drink. The rest said, Let be, let us see whether Elias will come to save him. Jesus, when he had cried again with a loud voice, yielded up the ghost. And, behold, the veil of the temple was rent in twain from the top to the bottom; and the earth did quake, and the rocks rent; And the graves were opened and many bodies of the saints which slept arose. And came out of the graves after his resurrection, and went into the holy city, and appeared unto many. Now when the centurion, and they that were with him, watching Jesus, saw the earthquake, and those things that were done, they feared greatly, saying, Truly this was the Son of God".

Literally, we are taught that the so-called "darkness" was a time of such blinding light that the people could not see. Esoterically, this "darkness" refers to the time when we are preparing to liberate ourselves from the "cross" of the body and are in "darkness" or doubt concerning the successful outcome. We are both fearful and somewhat uncertain.

We are also taught that Christ did not actually say, "My God, my God, Why hast thou forsaken me?", but that in reality He said, "My Father, for this cause was I brought into the world". This fact is not really important in that it does not effect the esoteric interpretation of our story, which is perhaps the main consideration of the writer of St. Matthew. He merely wishes the occult student to know through what experiences one must pass on the spiritual path.

Giving Christ the "reed" containing the sponge filled with vinegar represents a "bitterness" which the neophyte must not "accept" or "drink" after he has attained illumination. The "veil of the temple" is that "veil" or body which prevents us from gaining access to the higher planes until it is "rent". This "rending" of the "veil" represents a division of this vehicle or body which is necessary before Initiation is open to all. The "earthquake" is the jarring sensation or movement experienced by the person leaving his body when the spiritual vortices begin to spin prior to liberation from the body.

The "graves" symbolize materiality. Their opening indicates a release to the individual from the "darkness" and lack of understanding of the material viewpoint. The "saints" which were asleep in the graves represent the higher phases of the Initiate's own nature which have been "asleep" and which now are awakened through this liberation process. They "come out of their graves" or become active in those regions of the body in which they were formerly dormant. They "appear" to many, which means that many people are now able to see and feel their influence in and upon the one who has attained. The person himself also feels their effect powerfully. The "holy city" is a high state of consciousness into which these spiritual phases of the being go when they are awakened. Even the material mind (the centurion) is forced to acknowledge the divinity of the Christ after the startling demonstration at the Crucifixion.

"And many women were there beholding afar off, which

followed Jesus from Galilee, ministering unto him: Among which was Mary Magdalene, and Mary the mother of James and Joses, and the mother of Zebedee's children".

The women who follow Christ represent the feminine or emotional force which leaves the lower part of the body and ascends to the "place of the skull". It is said that Mary Magdalene was once a fallen woman. Esoterically, she would represent the emotional force, once used in the lower way, but now raised in regeneration.

"When the even was come, there came a rich man of Arimathæa, named Joseph, who also himself was Jesus's disciple: He went to Pilate, and begged the body of Jesus. Then Pilate commanded the body to be delivered. And when Joseph had taken the body, he wrapped it in a clean linen cloth. And laid it in his own new tomb, which he had hewn out in the rock: and he rolled a great stone to the door of the sepulchre, and departed. And there was Mary Magdalene, and the other Mary, sitting over against the sepulchre. Now the next day, that followed the day of preparation, the chief priests and Pharisees came together unto Pilate, Saying, Sir, we remember that that deceiver said, while he was yet alive, After three days I will rise again. Command therefore that the sepulchre be made sure until the third day, lest his disciples come by night, and steal him away, and say unto the people, He is risen from the dead: so the last error shall be worse than the first. Pilate said unto them, Ye have a watch: go your way, and make it as sure as ye can. So they went, and made the sepulchre sure, sealing the stone, and setting a watch".

Evening signifies the latter part of life, and with the majority of humanity attainment does not usually come until the life is almost finished. The rich man, in this instance, symbolizes one who is "rich" in spiritual attainment. Taking the body of Christ away from the authority of Pilate symbolizes the releasing of the spiritual nature from the dominance of the material mind. The wrapping of the body in a clean linen cloth indicates the great purity or spiritualization that had come to the physical being.

The new tomb which is hewn out of the rock represents the pineal gland, the spiritualization of which is part of the process of building the Philosopher's Stone. The Christ Force sets this gland into vibration through its contact. We believe that the rolling of the stone to the door of the sepulchre has the same meaning as "sealing the servants of God in their foreheads", as related in "Revelation".

The two Marys represent the higher and the lower emotional or feminine force, both used now constructively.

Formerly one was used in the lower way. Each neophyte has to raise both "Mary's" to the "place of the skull". The setting of the watch indicates that the mind places a mental guard before itself to keep it from accepting the Christ teachings. This guard which it sets up is predjudice, preconceived opinions and pride of intellect. There are other interpretations on other planes of consciousness concerning this part of the story.

CHAPTER 28.

"In the end of the sabbath, as it began to dawn toward the first day of the week, came Mary Magdalene and the other Mary to see the sepulchre. And behold, there was a great earthquake: for the angel of the Lord descended from heaven, and came and rolled back the stone from the door, and sat upon it. His countenance was like lightning, and his raiment was white as snow: And for fear of him the keepers did shake, and became as dead men. And the angel answered and said unto the women, Fear not ye: for I know that ye seek Jesus, which was crucified. He is not here: for he is risen, as he said. Come, see the place where the Lord lay. And go quickly, and tell his disciples that he is risen from the dead: and, behold, he goeth before you into Galilee; there shall ye see him: lo, I have told you. And they departed quickly from the sepulchre with fear and great joy; and did run to bring his disciples word. And as they went to tell his disciples, behold, Jesus met them, saying, All hail. And they came and held him by the feet, and worshipped him. Then said Jesus unto them, Be not afraid: go tell my brethren that they go into Galilee, and there shall they see me".

The coming of the two Marys to the sepulchre represents the raising of the Life Force to the pineal gland. The angel who rolled away the stone may symbolize that this gland had become active through divine power. The three days that Christ lay in the tomb represent approximately the time required to spiritualize the body through the conservation of the spiritual impulses which are said to be born each lunar month. A day corresponds to a year in this instance. The countenance of the angel being like lightning may describe the beauty of the awakened spiritual centers in the head. His raiment like "snow" describes the pure vehicles of the Initiate. As a result of these things happening within the neophyte, the material phases of being reverence God and the mind is no longer proud and harsh in its religion.

The command that the Disciples go into Galilee, and the Christ would meet them there describes the "travelling" or spreading of the Spirit throughout the entire body. The number of Disciples (twelve) symbolizes the fact that this Christ Force spiritualizes the seven centers of the desire body and the five centers of the vital body, which number twelve The fact that Christ had "risen" indicates, of course, the neophyte "raising" this Force. It also indicates that the neophyte has now become an Initiate, enters and leaves his body at will, and has "raised" his consciousness.

"Now when they were going, behold, some of the watch came into the city, and shewed unto the chief priests all the things that were done. And when they were assembled with the elders, and had taken counsel, they gave large money unto the soldiers, Saying, Say ye, His disciples came by night, and stole him away while we slept. And if this come to the governor's ears, we will persuade him and secure you. So they took the money, and did as they were taught: and this saying is commonly reported among the Jews until this day".

As we have said many times, the chief priests and elders represent phases of the mind. These verses show how difficult it is for the cold mind to accept the things of the Spirit. The Bible tells us that the imagination is evil from the day of our birth. It is the writer's belief that the mental phases of being are the last and most difficult to be converted. We are taught that in the latter days some of humanity will be frankly evil, regardless of many wonders which will be performed (as they were performed in our present story). These openly evil people will attempt to deceive themselves and others until the final day, just as the characters above have done.

"Then the eleven disciples went away into Galilee, into a mountain where Jesus had appointed them. And when they saw him, they worshipped him: but some doubted. And Jesus came and spake unto them, saying, All power is given unto me in heaven and earth. Go ye therefore, and teach all nations, baptizing them in the name of the Father, and of the Son, and of the Holy Ghost: Teaching them to observe all things whatsoever I have commanded you: and lo, I am with you alway, even unto the end of the world. Amen."

The mountain, as usual, symbolizes a lofty plane of consciousness, upon which the Disciples met the Christ. Some of them naturally doubted that it was the Christ, since the meeting took place on this high spiritual plane and their lack of familiarity with conditions there would cause a doubt. The newly-made Initiate has a hard time until he gets his bearings on these spiritual planes.

The Disciples are commanded to baptize in the name of the Father, the Son and the Holy Ghost. This may mean that they must draw down the power of the Triune God to be used in the purification process and the attainment of the power and spiritual illumination which this "baptizing" brings to the individual. The last words of the Christ given in St. Matthew are that we must enlighten others as well as to manifest in ourselves the spirituality of the three-fold God, so that all may become pure and Christ-like, and in time perform the same marvelous works that He Himself did. He tells us that in time we shall all become so pure and holy that we will be able to do even greater works than He did. But remember, dear reader, that when we have reached such a point, the Christ Himself will be doing still greater things, since evolution does not stand still. When an individual ceases to evolve, he crystallizes. This is contrary to spiritual evolution, which decrees that we must all go ONWARD AND UPWARD FOREVER.

The Gospel According to
ST. MARK

It is not the purpose of the writer to duplicate. For that reason, only those parts of St. Mark, St. Luke and St. John which bring out some new viewpoint that is not brought out clearly in St. Matthew, or some story not previously told, will be used. The writer does not attempt to give all of the esoteric meanings either in St. Matthew or the other Gospels, and for a definite reason. There are passages in which the physiological interpretation would not always be properly received. Also, it is not the purpose of the Rosicrucian Philosophy to dwell upon certain phases of life in detail. In other places the esoteric meanings are of such a nature that it would be dangerous for the casual reader to attempt to apply methods of development given. For those who wish all of the information possible, we suggest a careful study of all of the works of the great Initiate, Max Heindel.

There is little in St. Mark that is not found in St. Matthew. Nevertheless, certain points are brought out not previously explained.

The first story which brings additional information is the opening of the blind man's eyes by Christ. In St. Mark it is said that when the man's eyes were opened, he remarked that he saw men walking as trees. A moment later the man's sight is perfectly restored. As we have stated before, in the Bible "blindness" means spiritual blindness. When this man's eyes are opened, it is symbolic of the fact that he becomes spiritually awakened. There will be a time in the near future when we start becoming spiritual that we will also see men walking "as trees". This means that great changes will be made in humanity. At the present time man is the very opposite of the tree. He inhales oxygen and exhales carbon dioxide. The tree inhales carbon dioxide and exhales oxygen. We find the generative part of the plant or tree raised toward the Sun in beauty and gladness. We find the generative parts of Man held toward the earth in shame because of the misuse of the generative force. We find purity in the plant kingdom and impurity in the human kingdom. When Man's eyes become opened through contact with the Christ, he will cease his sinning and will "walk" in purity even as the trees and the plant kingdom. Then he shall indeed "see" with the pure eye of the Spirit as it was intended that he should.

Another new story brought out in St. Mark is the story of the widow and the two mites which she threw into the treasury. A "widow" represents the heart when it is not "wedded" to the material world. Neither is it "wedded" to the selfish, self-seeking mind. Therefore, when the pure heart gives, it is like the offering of Abel, which is acceptable to God, since it gives of itself with its material offering. The heart gives with love, which is a product of the heart. Meditate upon this if you are inclined to be coldly intellectual. Let us remember that all of these stories must take place within ourselves. Our hearts must become "widows" and lose the "wedded to the things of the earth" attitude, and then its gifts, which may seem as small as the two mites of the widow to the intellectualist, may be very large in the eyes of divinity, which see the love that goes with the gift. God is not in need of money, since the cattle on a thousand hills are His, and the hills also. We believe that the spiritual hierarchies who work for God and try to help us want only our love and our purity.

St. Mark also brings out a little more clearly the description of the man in whose house Christ is to spend the Passover. The Disciples are told to follow a man bearing a pitcher of water on his shoulder and that he will conduct them to an upper chamber where a feast will be prepared. The man bearing the pitcher of water on his shoulder symbolizes the man of the New Age who will have perfect control over the "Water of Life" (the Life Force). We must follow the ideal as represented by this man, and when we do he will "conduct" us to the "upper chamber" (the head) where this raised Force will open our consciousness to the heaven worlds and give us the spiritual "feast" which is prepared for those who will follow the ideals of the Aquarian Age.

The story of the young man who fled when the multitude came to take Christ is interpreted in this manner: It will be remembered that when they laid hands on him (the young man) he fled and left his garment with the multitude. The young man represents Innocence. This innocence was maintained until he became a part of the destructive multitude. Then, they, through contact with him, took away his "garment" or caused his downfall. We suggest the reading of Kipling's "If" in this connection. We think the line, "If you can walk with crowds and keep your virtue", applies here. Let us each meditate upon this story and strive to maintain our poise as much in the crowds and the "marketplace" as in the "desert" or secluded place where we are not tempted and contaminated by the "crowd".

We are indebted to St. Mark for giving us the proper definition of a Christian. The term, "Christian", is so greatly misunderstood that in the past, and some times even now, when a minister or an evangelist would ask those in the congregation who were Christians to raise their hands, everyone would do so. Their intentions were good. We all *want* to be Christians, but it requires work as well as faith to make one a Christian according to St. Mark. He says that the following signs shall follow those who believe in Christ and are therefore Christians: They shall cast out devils; they shall speak with new tongues; they shall take up serpents, and if they drink any deadly thing, it shall not hurt them; they shall lay hands on the sick and they shall recover. I wonder how many of us can qualify as Christians according to this real definition of the word. It might be interesting to know why a true Christian can do these things. A very good explanation is given on Page 20 of "Revelation, Esoterically Interpreted" by the writer.

In the description of the temptation of Christ in the wilderness, St. Mark says that He was with "wild beasts". St. Matthew uses the word "devil" in this connection. "Wild beasts", of course, describes the animal nature within each of us before it has been subdued. This is the experience of each neophyte who must conquer and subdue the "wild beasts" of his being in the "wilderness" or during the period of preparation. Both "wilderness" and "desert" have the same symbolical meaning. They signify a time of spiritual preparation, since both places are devoid of the "weights" of civilization which hold us to this earth. The neophyte does not literally have to go to a desert to prepare himself. He will become stronger if he can continue to live in the world and yet not be a part of it. It is much easier to conquer the selfish phases of life in seclusion than it is in the place where there are many temptations.

St. Mark gives us the story of the sick man who was not able to contact Christ until the tiles of the roof had been broken up and he had been let down through the top of the house. Many of us are not able to contact Christ until we have broken up the crystallized condition of our minds—our preconceived opinions and old ideas. When the "tiles" have been "broken up" in our minds, then the "sick" man within each of us can contact the Christ through the spiritual enlightenment of the mind. Some people are able to contact the Christ through the heart and some through the mind, as brought out in various incidents in the story of His life. The Bible emphasizes the fact that there are two types of people, the occult and the mystic.

Another incident in St. Mark is that in which the Disciples are told to bring the colt upon which Christ is to ride into Jerusalem. It is tied in "a place by the door without where two ways meet". This "colt" is again the lower animal force by which power the "Christ" ascends to the higher consciousness or the "Jerusalem". The fact that the colt is "tied", in one sense, signifies that this power has never been used as it is now to be. That it is "tied without the door" shows that it has not yet entered into the spinal canal. This Force may be used either for regeneration or degeneration, and thus it stands "at the crossways" or "where two ways meet". It may either be raised upward for illumination or downward in sensuality. This fact is well expressed symbolically when it is said that the colt is tied in a place "where two ways meet". Thus we see that St. Mark goes more into detail concerning some of the incidents in the life of Christ. He also leaves out much in other places which are brought out in St. Matthew. We find descriptions of additional visitations of Christ after the Resurrection which are not found in St. Matthew. For a scientific explanation of the appearance of the Master, going through closed doors, etc., read the "Cosmo Conception".

The Gospel According to ST. LUKE

Our first new story in this Gospel is that of Zacharias, the priest, and Elizabeth, his wife. This is a story that must be enacted within each of us before the story of the union of Joseph and Mary can take place within. The reason is that John, the child of Zacharias and Elizabeth, represents mental enlightenment. This mental birth must naturally take place within (especially if we are of the occult type) before the spiritualization of the heart or emotional nature, represented by Christ. The mind must be made active first and then prepare the way for the spiritualization of the heart. The heart, however, will eventually become a power greater than the mind.

Zacharias became dumb before his child was born. We are all "dumb" in a spiritual sense before the birth of the enlightened mind. Zacharias and his wife were old people, which bears out the fact that it is usually not until the follies of youth are passed that we learn real wisdom and understanding.

It was the duty of Zacharias to burn incense in the temple. This signifies that we must continually send up the pure, sweet "incense" of sanctification in the body (the "temple") before the birth of the "John" within can be accomplished. In other words, we must purify ourselves or "burn incense in the temple of the Lord" in preparation for the spiritual enlightenment of the mind.

In St. Luke we are told plainly and undeniably that John was the reincarnated Elias, who had returned to earth to try to influence the disobedient children of Israel to accept God. The fact that an angel appeared to Zacharias and told him about the coming birth of John indicates that we will establish contact with the spiritual worlds and receive many messages before our minds finally become purified. Let the writer urge the reader to make these contacts under a Western system or a positive school. We are Westerners and the Western Wisdom Teachings are best suited for our development. This helps us to be masters of ourselves on the inner planes, which is not always possible when a Westerner attempts to develop through an Eastern school.

The angel who gave this message to Zacharias was Gabriel. It is logical that he should be the messenger because he is the ambassador of the angelic life wave to our earth. The angels inhabit the Moon and have charge of generation.

Gabriel and his angels always fortell a physical birth, since it is their work to assist us to bring Egos to birth in this world.

Later Gabriel also appears to Mary and tells her of the coming birth of Jesus. This again emphasizes the fact that the enlightened mind must be born first before the purification of the heart takes place, symbolized by the birth of Jesus. Mary was a virgin, and the "Jesus" within can only be born to the pure or virgin heart. Certainly it cannot be born to a heart that is full of material and sensual desires.

Gabriel tells Mary that the Holy Ghost will overshadow her. This is literally true. The Holy Ghost or Jehovah has charge of generation and the physical birth of Egos. However, this does not mean that the Initiate husband, Joseph, a man capable of helping to produce a child without the passion incident to generation, did not unite with the Virgin Mary to bring to birth the Initiate, Jesus. Jesus was later to furnish the physical body through which the great Christ Spirit functioned while on earth.

With the birth of John, the mouth of Zacharias was opened and he was able to speak. Until this takes place within each of us we may say words but they are not full of wisdom. Our minds have to become purified or the old consciousness (Zacharias) united with the heart (Elizabeth), which gives birth to the new consciousness. When this takes place, our words will begin to have real wisdom. The child, John, was in the desert (place of preparation) until his presentation in Israel. This symbolizes that even after the mind becomes spiritualized it must go through a period of preparation before it reaches its ultimate strength.

Next the story of the birth of Jesus is told, which is practically the same as in the other Gospels. The journey of the shepherds (keepers of purity) from the various fields (parts of the body) to the manger or birthplace of Jesus represents the following of the "Star" within. All occult students at a certain point in their work learn to "follow-the star". He learns to liberate himself from his cramped position in the physical body, which, in one sense, constitutes a "birth" to the spiritual planes.

"Every male that openeth the womb shall be called holy to the Lord". Male here symbolizes a product of the mind or a thought, which is represented as being masculine because the mind from which it comes is masculine in its nature. This sentence means that every thought born to us (which "opens the womb") should be holy or sacred to God, for under Cosmic law we must account for every idle word and for every thought.

There is a story of a just man named Simeon, who is told by the Holy Ghost that he shall not die until he holds the Christ child in his arms. The just man, Simeon, represents each of us when we become just and pure. We shall be "told" or become aware through the Holy Ghost phase of the God Within, of the coming birth of the Christ Within long before it takes place. The spiritualization of the Holy Ghost principle within us naturally precedes the birth of the next higher principle, the Christ Within. Simeon tells Mary that Jesus is to save Israel. Israel means "Light" and the above is symbolic of the fact that after the Christ Within is born, He will spiritualize or "save" the higher faculties of the being (represented by Israel) from being destroyed by the animal nature.

Simeon tells Mary that her heart will be pierced also. This means that the heart or emotional nature of each of us must suffer before the path of the "Christ Child" within finally leads to "Golgotha" and we are freed from the body to travel the higher worlds in the service of humanity.

The story of the Christ Child in the temple is one that has not been told before. This incident in which the Christ teaches the learned men in the temple tells us that we must all raise the Christ Within so that he becomes strong enough to make His influence felt in the "temple" or the body. The five teachers represent the five physical senses. When we have raised this "Christ Child" within us, we shall intuitively and spiritually receive sermons which are far above the teachings that we have formerly received through the five senses. These five senses were, until the coming of Christ, the "teachers in the temple", but when they hear the words of the "Christ Child", they are amazed. His teachings are much deeper than can be comprehended through the senses. They of themselves are not able to understand the teachings of the newly-awakened Christ Wisdom.

John was responsible for teaching the people that they must no longer think they are a chosen people merely because of Abraham or other of their ancestors who were close to God. He tells them that it is the work of the individual which brings salvation to a person, regardless of who his or her ancestors were.

The next piece of information that we do not find in St. Matthew or St. Mark exactly as given in St. Luke is the geneology which is supposed to have been the lineal descent of Jesus. The interpretation of these names may seem to the reader rather as though we were straining a point to make a story out of them. This is because, in the midst of the story, the Bible writer injects names not necessary to the main story, but for the purpose of giving glory and praise to God. It is as though a minister in the midst of his sermon frequently interrupts the trend of his sermon to give praise and glory to God. Another confusing thing is that in places the names are so arranged that they must be read backwards, or from effect to cause, instead of from cause to effect, (or rather that the *meaning* of the names must be read backwards). This is probably to give a hint concerning our own Life Cycle where, on a certain plane, our own life story is unrolled backwards or from effect to cause.

Jesus ("God is salvation") is produced in us through, or is the "son" of Joseph ("a budding rod"), who is the son of Heli ("my God"). Thus, we are told that God (both within and without) brings salvation to us through regeneration, which causes the Life Force to ascend the spinal cord. This causes it to "bud" and bring the enlightenment and wisdom incident to this process of spiritualization.

(The above geneology begins at the twenty-third verse of the third chapter of St. Luke).

Heli comes from (is the "son" of) Matthat ("a gift") which is produced by (or is the "son" of) Levi ("joined"). Thus, we are told that this spiritual gift only comes from "joining" ourselves to, or using the gift of, the power that is of, and comes from, God.

Here the writer digresses for a moment in order to express his thankfulness to God for the privilege of regeneration. This is expressed by four names, Melchi, Janna, Joseph and Mattathias. We believe the writer wishes to tell us that "Jehovah is my king" (Melchi) and "Jehovah has been gracious" (Janna) in the matter of the "budding rod" (Joseph) which is a great "gift" (Mattathias) to mankind. Thus we stop and praise God with the writer for the opportunity or "gift" given us to raise the Life Force up the "rod" of the spinal cord in regeneration, causing the latent pineal gland and pituitary body to "bud" into activity and flower into spiritual enlightenment and illumination.

Again the geneology seems to resolve itself into an inserted story that this time takes eight names. We start with Amos ("bearer of a burden") and we find ourselves indeed bearing many burdens until we learn to throw off the many weights that hold us to the material world. Amos is the son of Naum ("comforter"), and we know the Father will "comfort" us and help us to raise ourselves from the sorrow caused by our sins. The next name is Esli ("God has reserved"), who comes from Nagge ("brightness"), who is the son of Maath ("small"), who comes from Mattathais ("gift"), who comes from Semei ("name", "fame", etc.), which comes from

Joseph ("the fruitful vine" or "the budding rod"). Thus this story tells us, in these eight names, that although we will have "burdens", we will be "comforted" through a "small", "bright" "gift" "that God has reserved" for us, when we cause the "vine" to become "fruitful" or the " rod" to "bud"—and this will bring us a "name" or "fame" (high vibration). A "name" is a vibration, and the fact that this name is one of "fame" signifies a high spiritual vibration. Thus we are told that when we cause the "vine" of the spinal cord to become fruitful through regeneration, it will cause the small, bright pineal gland to become active, which will bring us as a gift from God the spiritual light that will comfort and relieve us from our spiritual burdens. This will cause us to have the name and reputation of a saint or a true follower of God.

It appears in the next story that the writer of the Book of St. Luke wishes to drive home a lesson through repetition. The story is told in twelve names. They are, Juda ("praised"), Joanna ("God is good"), Rhesa ("chieftain"), Zorobabel ("begotten in Babylon"), Salathiel ("I ask God"), Neri ("God is my lamp"), Melchi ("Jehovah is my king") Addi ("ornament"), Cosam ("seer"), Elmodan ("God is loved") Er ("watchful"), and Jose ("he shall add" or "fruitful vine" or "budding rod"). These names tell us to "praise God", who is "good", and learn to bring forth the Christ Force in "Babylon", where we are captives to the physical senses. We become "chieftans", however, when we "ask God", who is our "lamp" and "spiritual light". He causes the "ornament" (pineal gland) to shine in spiritual brightness. If we are "watchful" and careful, He will "add" to our spiritual understanding and cause the light to shine in the former darkness of our "temple" of being. "Let there be light".

The reader must remember that in the apparent repetition many times of almost the same story, that it is an occult custom to do this for the sake of emphasis. Many illustrative stories are told in which the neophyte knocks three times upon the door, or asks the sage the same question three times, or returns three times, before his patience is rewarded by an answer. Persistence is a spiritual virtue. Repetition is an occult method of making an impression upon the vital body.

The names which form our next story are, Eliezer ("God is help'), Jorim ("God is exalted"), Matthat ("gift"), Levi ("joined"), Simeon ("hearkening"), Juda ("praised"), Joseph ("fruitful bow"), Jonan ("God has been gracious"), Eliakim ("God establishes"), Melea ("fullness"), Menan (?), and Mattatha ("a gift"). These names tell us to "praise and exalt God. It promises that we will receive a "gift" if we will "join" or "unite" with God and "hearken" or "listen" ("praise God"), for God has given us the "gift" and privilege of attaining the "fullness" of spirituality through the "fruitful bow" that we may cultivate. Thus, God gives us the gift or privilege of establishing ourselves spiritually and bringing to ourselves every good and perfect thing, when we hearken to His word, regenerate ourselves and approach His holy throne.

The next story found in the list of ancestors of Jesus is almost identically the same story that we find in the back of the Book of Ruth. It might be interesting for the reader to see how one Bible writer substantiates another in this way. For an interesting comparison, turn to the last two pages of "Ruth, Esoterically Interpreted" by the writer. You will find the same story told and interpreted as we find here, with slight variations. Our names here are, Nathan ("a gift"), David ("beloved of God"), Jesse ("a gift"), Obed ("to worship"), Boaz ("strength"), Salmon ("a garment"), Naasson ("alchemist"), Aminadab ("kin of princes"), Aram ("a country among the rivers"), Esrom ("a dwelling"), Phares ("a break"), Juda ("praised"), Jacob ("supplanter"), Isaac ("joy"), Abraham ("father of a multitude").

Beginning at the proper end of this story (Abraham), we find humanity starting with God, Who is the "father of a multitude". We know that it was not one couple but humanity as a whole who were differentiated within the "Father". We lived in "joy" (Isaac) in the heaven worlds or "Garden of Eden" until the "supplanter" (Jacob), which represents the time when the Lucifer Spirits came in and "supplanted" the "spiritual" or "praised" (Juda) consciousness, appeared and caused a "break" (Phares) in our normal or intended evolution. From this "break" we were driven from the "Garden" and came to make our "dwelling" (Esrom) in physical bodies in this physical world, where we were "shut in" to the material consciousness and shut out of the spiritual consciousness. Esrom also means "shut in".

Next we have the word, Aram, which tells quite a story in itself. Aram means "certain districts in Syria and Mesopotamia". Mesopotamia means "among the rivers" or "the country of the two rivers". Syria was a country along the eastern coast of the Mediterranean, and extending inland to Mesopotamia. The capital of Syria was Damascus, which was called "the most ancient city in the world". A city symbolizes a state of consciousness. If the reader will put these meanings together, he will see that the country of, or place of, "the two rivers" in the eastern part or "front" of the body has to do with the masculine and feminine attributes of sex, which are located in that part of the body. Damascus, the capital, being the "oldest city in the world" or oldest state of consciousness, indicates that the consciousness of sex, or the consciousness caused through sex, is the "oldest" or first physical consciousness of mankind. (We know that it was the original sin that brought about our first physical consciousness and lost for us our spiritual consciousness and contact with the heaven worlds). Thus, in the one word, Aram, we are told that the first consciousness of primitive mankind was caused through sexual contact at the time the two separate sexes manifested. This took place after we had changed from our original dual-sexed condition. (We were first dual-sexed, as we were made in the image of God.). We are now in that temporary phase of evolution when separateness is at its greatest height. Therefore, mankind has lost one polarity. The time will come in the far future when we will again enjoy both polarities, and sex as we know it will be a thing of the past.

After we found ourselves "shut in" the material world, we longed for the "Father's house" again. We began to climb back with the help of spiritual beings (Aminadab means "kin of princes"), and these higher "kin" or "princes" to whom we are related spiritually, assisted us in our climb. With their assistance, we became spiritual "alchemists" (Naasson). We are even now building the "golden wedding garment" (Salmon means "a garment"). When we have built this spiritual vehicle in which to function in the "Garden of Eden" or heaven worlds again, we will have become spiritually strong (Boaz means "strength"). We will then make a "gift" (Jesse) of ourselves in the service of humanity. We will then become "David", which means "beloved of God". This indicates that we will have become great saints in power and spirit, through service. All of this is through the grace of the "gift" (Nathan) given us in the form of the life in which we live and move and have our being, all of which is a "gift" from God.

We believe that the next message intended is that the Christ vibration is the force that will cause a branch to sprout, that will bring fellowship to this world of dissension and division, and will cause this "one with the branch" to become a friend of God. He will "spring up" into the vibration of Initiation. In better English: we are told in this story that the Christ Force will build within us the "rod" which "buds". This spiritualization of the spinal cord and pituitary and pineal glands, will bring love and fellowship into our hearts. instead of the selfish, cold divisions we have today among mankind. This change will make the regenerated one a friend of God and will carry him to spiritual heights that will mean consciousness on a higher plane or Initiation. This is what we believe the writer of the book intends to convey to the deeper student who is searching for some meaning in this long list of names used in the lineage of Jesus.

Sem means a "name" or a vibration and Arphaxad, the next word, is the son of Sem. The Christ is the Son of the Father vibration or spiritual power. This is the force or "worker" (Cainan means "artificer" or "smith") that will cause a "branch" (Sala) to sprout. This will produce "fellowship" (Heber) in this world of division (Phalec). This will cause "the one with the branch" to become a "friend of God" (Ragau). He will "spring up" (Saruch) into the "vibration" (Nachor) of "Initiation" (Thara, a "plane" or "station,").

It will be noted that St. Matthew and St. Luke do not use the same names in the geneology, though both are sup posed to be giving the same line of descent. Whenever two Bible writers disagree or apparently contradict each other, then is the time for the spiritual student to study carefully. An apparnet contradiction is usually made for the purpose of calling attention to the contradiction, so that the deeper student in his meditation will receive messages from both and each will complement the other.

The last message in this geneological line carries ten names. They are, Adam, Seth, Enos, Cainan, Maleleel, Jared, Enoch, Mathusala, Lamech, and Noe. The meaning concealed is that in the beginning humanity (Adam) were pure in heart (Seth) and lived in the higher consciousness, but eventually became manlike (Enos). We made (Cainan means "make"), "praise God" (Maleleel), our descent (Jared). We acquired wisdom (Enoch) by conquering (Mathusala) the "destroyer" (Lamech) and attained Initiation (Noe). The reader can readily see how these names work themselves out logically in the natural development of mankind. Adam means humanity. Seth means the pure heart or represents us as we were in the beginning. Enos means a "man", such as we became later. Cainan means a "smith" or one who causes work to be done. Maleleel means "praise of God". Jared means "descent" and Enoch means "wisdom". Mathusala means "man of a dart", or "one who conquers". Lamech means "the destroyer", which is the lower use of the Lift Force. Noe or Noah is the one who builds the "ark", soul body or "golden wedding garment" that allows him to rise above "flood waters" of passion and rest his "ark" upon the mount of Initiation. He learns not to send out "ravens" (dark thoughts) but to send out "doves" (pure thoughts). These return with the "olive branch" of peace. This tells us that when we arrive at that pure stage as symbolized by

Noah, we will send out only love and pure thoughts. They will come back to us, even as the love and spiritual vibrations sent out by the angels return to them.

In St. Luke, Christ tells us that when the heavens were "shut up" three years and six months, Elias was sent only to a widow at Sarepta, a city of Sidon. This may be a hint to us that our own higher consciousness is "shut off", for this same period of time, during which the being is regenerated. During this period of regeneration spiritual "seeds" or impulses said to be born each lunar month are raised to the "Jerusalem" or the head. Elias represents the spiritualized mind, and the widow represents the heart or emotional nature which has separated itself from the allurements of the world. This is the meaning of "widow" in the esoteric sense. There is naturally a great "famine" when the heavens are shut up, since it is always a spiritual famine that comes to us when we shut ourselves away from the higher life. Sidon means "fishing" and Sarepta is asociated with "burning". Therefore, these two words describe the fact that the Spinal Spirit Fire carries the little "fish" or seed up the spinal canal. This requires the "burning" or sacrificing of the lower self for the sake of the higher.

Christ tells the people that there were many lepers in the time of Eliseus (Elisha), but that Eliseus was sent only to Naaman, the Syrian. Naaman was a eunuch. From the occult interpretation, this means that he did not abuse the Life Force or practice sensuality. Therefore, Elisha (a representative of God) was able to come to him and heal him of his disease. It is impossible for any of us to overcome our karma until we have throughly learned our lesson in connection with it. Naaman had done this when he became a "eunuch" for the "kingdom of heaven's sake". This does not mean, however, that the individual must literally emasculate himself, but that he must in time become a spiritual "eunuch" and use the Life Force physically only to bring an Ego into the world and not for sensuality.

Naaman was a Syrian. If the reader will refer to the interpretation of Aram given previously, he will obtain additional evidence of the fact that Naaman had control of the lower nature. In the interpretation of Aram, it is mentioned that Syria has for its capital Damascus, the "oldest city in the world". Damascus represents the type of consciousness that gives the key to the story. We suggest that the reader turn back to this interpretation of Aram.

We next find the story in which Jesus tells Simon to let down his net, after he had been toiling all night and had caught nothing. When he does this, he catches so many fish that his net breaks. He calls to his friends in a second ship to help him. They fill both the ships with the fish until they nearly sink. The esoteric significance of this story is that when we are endeavoring to raise those who are living in the lower emotions ("fish") above the "waters" to a higher plane of thinking, we toil in "darkness" or ignorance until the Christ comes. With Him to guide us in the work we are better able to interest and help those who are in need. Before His coming we have been toiling in ignorance, but after illumination from Him, we have the light of understanding in our hearts and minds to aid us in our spiritual work.

The raising of the young man of Nain, the son of a widow, who was dead, simply describes the raising through Initiation of a young man who was "dead" to the allurements of the world. One must "die" to material things before he can be raised to a consciousness of the spiritual life. The word Nain has to do with clairvoyance. The reader can easily see that this story parallels the Masonic legend in which the candidate is a "son of a widow" and must be "raised" from the "dead" or the horizontal position to the upright through the strong grip of the "Lion of Judah". In the Bible story it is describing a real spiritual Initiation in which the candidate receives illumination.

Another story found in St. Luke and not in the other Gospels is the incident in which the Disciples forbade a man to cast out devils in the name of Christ because this man did not follow with them. Christ said, "Forbid him not: for he that is not against us is for us". Too often the various religious sects fight one another because each wishes to be considered greater, not perceiving that they are all on the same road and striving for the same goal.

In the above story it is brought out that there is only one power in the world and that is the Life of God, in which we live and move and have our being. There is only one Force with which we can "cast out devils". This is the Life of God. Bear in mind, however, that this Force may be used either for good or evil. The difference between a white magician and a black magician is the way in which each uses the Force.

The story of the man who came from Jerusalem to Jerico is very illustrative and has not been previously given. This is a description of the consciousness falling from the spiritual to the material. The man in this story falls among thieves. This is very logical. When the consciousness is lowered to unworthy things, these things "rob" one of all that is worth while.

While he is in this condition and sorely wounded the Levite and the Priest pass him by without helping him.

This indicates that there is no real help for us in mere religion of form or intellectual religion. The Samaritan comes and binds up his wounds, takes him to the inn and has him cared for at his own expense. The Samaritan, although he is one of the lower classes or despised people of this country, is nevertheless the real "neighbour". He represents the constructive use of the Life Force, or the "living" religion. This is the actual working of the physiological law of God and is the only thing which will heal our wounds and bring us back to the "inn" or the "house of the Father".

The story of Mary and Martha follows. Mary sits at the feet of Christ, while Martha complains that she is forced to do all of the work. This brings out several principles. One is that when we choose to sink the consciousness into material things, we shall find life becoming more and more tedious. There are very few rich persons whose worldly possessions are not a care to them. On the other hand, those who sit at the feet of Christ will find that their hearts are free from care and full of love and happiness.

The second principle revealed in this story (to the sincere student) is that we must fulfill all material obligations before we are free to give our time to the higher side of life. Mary represents those of us who have no karma or material obligations to prevent concentrating almost entirely on spiritual things. Martha represents those of us who cannot spend all our time at the feet of Christ because we have yet unfulfilled debts to work out. Let us all, therefore, endeavor to work out our karma through "loving, self-forgetting service". We shall then be privileged in time to play the part of Mary, for rest assured that we will not be so privileged until we have paid all karmic debts which may interfere.

When the woman would bless the womb that bare Jesus and the "paps that gave him suck", we are to understand that it is to the spiritual rather than to the physical which we must look. Christ said, "Yea, rather, blessed are they that hear the word of God and keep it".

We are told in St. Luke to let our "loins be girded about" or to restrain the lower nature; to "let our lower lights be burning", and so light the seven spiritual centers of the desire body and the five of the vital body. We are told that the tower of Siloam fell on eighteen men who were no more wicked than the others. The time had come when these eighteen men must pay their karma. Our karma will also be due at the proper time. Unless we restrain our "loins" and stop creating fresh karma, and start paying off what we already owe through loving service, we, like the men of Siloam, will have a severe day of reckoning.

St. Luke tells us that the unfruitful tree is to be given one more chance; that the gardener will fertilize it and give it every possible attention, and then if it does not produce, it will be cast away. The unfruitful tree represents those of us who are violating Cosmic law and falling behind in evolution. Extra care will be given us in the form of a better explanation of Cosmic law and more advanced teachings concerning it. After due pains have been taken with us and we still do not respond, we shall be forced to drop back in evolution and wait for a new school of life, since we can be lost to the present one if we do not progress satisfactorily.

The story of the Pharisees coming to the Christ and telling Him that Herod will kill Him while He is not in Jerusalem, finds the Christ replying that it is impossible for a prophet to perish out of Jerusalem. This means that Herod, the lower nature can only kill the Christ Force through the mind. If one is to kill out the higher, it is through the mind that this is done. Jerusalem (representing, now, the mind) is the place where all the "prophets" have been killed, because when Herod, the lower nature, has control of "Jerusalem", the mind, it is natural that the "prophets" or higher phases of being will be killed out.

Christ stresses the value of humility in the story of the man who tries to sit in the highest seat at the wedding feast. This man endeavored to usurp more power and fame than his vibration warranted. Another came who really was entitled to honors, and the impostor was forced in shame to descend in the estimation of all. There are many lecturers and teachers who claim to possess great powers. The people not having the proper development to perceive the falseness of their claims, take them at their word. In time a true teacher comes along and the impostors are discovered and humiliated.

Let us take heed from this story and try always to be humble. Let us not pretend to a spiritual development greater than we actually possess, for sooner or later we shall be properly catalogued. If we remain humble, we shall eventually find the work and position which is commensurate with our true spiritual standing.

Christ tells us that when we give of our bounty, to give to them who cannot repay us, so that our bounty will be of the most good. We must consider carefully the cost of both a spiritual and a material career. We must consider exactly what is required in each case and the results of each type of existence, rather than to walk blindly down the road of life. Salt is good, but when it has lost its savor, it is no longer tasty. A chosen people, if they do not continue to develop, will not remain a chosen people. A swift runner may be able to win the race, but if he does not keep up his pace and if he stops too often to rest, another will come from behind, pass him, and become the favored one in his stead. There is no standing still in the great race of evolution that leads from the clod to God.

The parable of the Prodigal Son is another story found in St. Luke which is left out of St. Matthew and St. Mark. In this story, the younger son, to whom the father gives his portion or inheritance, represents the human life wave. The long journey of the younger son from his father's home represents the long descent made by humanity from the "Garden of Eden" or the spiritual state enjoyed by humanity at the beginning of its evolution, to its immersion in the dense physical world. During its career in the material world humanity (the prodigal son) wastes its substance or "inheritance" (the Life Force) in riotous living. This is a result of taking generation into its own hands. Then comes a famine (a spiritual famine) as a result of which mankind lost contact with spiritual things. The prodigal son feeds the "swine", which indicates that humanity was "feeding" the animalistic phases of its being through sensual living. It finally sees the misery of such an existence and resolves to return unto the "Father's house", the heaven worlds. The Father will naturally "come to meet him". God always comes more than half way to meet us when we endeavor to return to His ways. At the home-coming, the best robe is put upon the prodigal son. This represents the "golden wedding garment", the spiritual vehicle which we shall all build and wear at some future time during the return to the "Father's house". The shoes which are placed on the younger son's feet symbolize the power to "travel" on the astral planes. It also signifies the purification of those nerves and centers in the feet.

The ring which is placed on the younger sons's finger symbolizes that humanity will have achieved the alchemical marriage within the self, where the heart and the head will become "wedded" or joined in the spiritual balance of the masculine and feminine poles of being. The "fatted calf", of course, is the phase of being which was formerly misused, the animal self, and which now becomes the spiritual food absorbed or "eaten" by humanity at this period.

The complaint of the older brother brings out an interesting point. The older brother represents the angelic life wave. He complains that the father never killed the fatted calf for him, nor gave him any special banquet, nor made a great rejoicing for him. The father replies that it is because he (the older son) has always been with him. This means that the angelic wave has always remained with the Father in the spiritual worlds. They had never made a descent into matter or the "swine-pen" as had humanity. Naturally, everything that is the Father's has always been theirs.

The parable of the unjust steward teaches that when we do a thing, we should do it wholeheartedly. When the unjust steward found that his lord was going to take away his position, he arranged with his lord's creditors to cheat him in order that he might have favor with the creditors. Christ says that this at least shows consistency. If we are going to be evil, it is better to make our friendships with those who are evil, since assuredly, God will have no place for us.

The Bible tells us to do that which we do with all our might. This advice is thoroughly occult. When we do wrong if we do it with all of our strength, the penalty we shall have to pay will be so severe that we will not likely do wrong so easily next time. The suffering we will experience will prevent our committing the same mistake so easily again. On the other hand, when we do good, the joy we will experience, if we do this good with all of our might, will be so great that we will be impelled to do again that which causes us so much happiness. But when we do things half-heartedly, we receive neither sufficient joy nor sufficient punishment to make a very great impression, and therefore the experience is not of much value.

In St. Luke there is told the parable of the rich man who dined sumptiously every day and the beggar Lazarus, that lay at his door. They both died and the rich man went to hell and Lazarius to heaven. When the rich man begged that Lazarius come to comfort him, he was told that he could not. Neither could he go to warn his brethren on earth. It was said that if they would not listen to the living, they would not listen to the dead.

The moral of this story is obvious. Those who are rich in a material sense may be very poor spiritually; and *vice versa*. There are indeed deep gulfs on the other planes. We are like balloons with ballast. Our low vibrations or "weights" hold us to the lower planes, while those who have rid themselves of the "weights" which so easily beset us, naturally gravitate to the higher planes. It is very objectionable for those who are pure, after they have passed on, to come down to the lower planes on which we dwell. This may be proven to the reader by the fact that when his loved ones pass on in death, he "dreams" about them frequently at first, but later less and less. That is because, as they gradually go through the period of purification which must take place after death, it becomes more and more objectionable for the so-called "dead" to visit their loved ones in the lower vibration of the earth. Therefore, they meet less and less often in "dreams". Finally, they meet no more at all.

The story of the ten lepers who were healed, and of the one who turned back to give thanks, exactly describes the condition of mankind today. Mankind receives the great gifts of life and love, etc. from God, but very seldom gives thanks in return for the privilege of enjoying these blessings. It is also clearly brought out that only those who give thanks and change their ways of living from the material to the spiritual will remain permanently "clean". We will bring back upon ourselves the results of our sins in the end, though at first, or for a time, we may seem to be cured.

The moral to the story of the Pharisee and the publican who pray is the same as that given at length in the Sixth Chapter of St. Matthew. The reader is advised to refer to the interpretation of this chapter of St. Matthew. It is also suggested that he read the novel, "Magnificent Obsession" by Lloyd Douglas. The moral in brief is that the person who prays that he may be heard gets no credit with God, since he gets full credit on earth. The publican who prayed sincerely in his heart and abased himself was heard "in secret" by God and was exalted on earth.

The story of the widow crying for revenge is the story of the heart that will never be satisfied as long as we break God's laws. Therefore, the judge, who represents the mind, decides to avenge her, or do justice to the heart because of its continual cries to him. Even though he, the judge, may not be interested in God, the continual cries and longings of the unsatisfied heart compel him to take action. Christ says that there are many who live right just for this reason. There is much ground for meditation here, as worth while principles are revealed.

The next story not found in the previous Gospels is the story of Zacchæus. He was a small man and he had to climb a sycamore tree in order to see Christ pass on His way to Jerusalem. Those of us who are "small" in spiritual stature must "climb the sycamore tree" or cause the spinal force to ascend the spinal canal. Then we will be able to "see" Christ when He comes into the "Jerusalem" of our being. Jerusalem symbolizes the head or the "dome of the temple" or the higher consciousness. We will be told on that day, as Christ told Zacchæus, "This day will I abide at thy house". This is literally true. When we "climb" the "tree" of being with the Christ Force, it will come and "sup" with us in the "upper room" of the "house", or in other words, the head.

The two thieves who were crucified with the Christ are said to represent the head and the heart. The thief representing the head reviled the Christ. The one who represents the heart repented and begged the Christ to remember him when

He came into His kingdom. It is through the heart that we repent, and it is the heart which shall be our salvation. The Christ promises to remember the thief who repents. The heart or emotional nature, at times, may be well-described as a "thief". This is when, through generating sensual emotions, it "steals" the use of the Life Force. When it repents it will receive forgiveness and will ultimately be in Paradise, after the debts of its sins have been paid. However, forgiveness alone does not cancel a debt. Even though the thief was forgiven by the Christ, he still had his bones broken and went through the awful tortures of the crucifixion.

In St. Luke the description of the appearances of the Christ differs from that given in the previous Gospels. This does not give us a great deal more of esoteric information. Although some interpreters of the Bible make much of this difference, we only stress the importance of the fact that Christ *did* appear after the Crucifixion to His Disciples. The Twelve Disciples symbolize twelve attributes within ourselves, and the Christ represents the Spirit Within. When this spiritual self or "Christ" has been liberated from the body it will indeed "appear" and talk to the "Twelve Disciples" or will come to us in the "upper chamber" (the head) and will expound the Scriptures and the mysteries of life to us, if we may hear the sweet voice of the Spirit.

Note: Judas Iscariot was one of the original Twelve. This is as it should be, since we all start with "Judas Iscariot" (the "thief") who "carries the bag" and finally "hangs" himself after betraying the Spirit Within. After the death of this lower quality, it is only proper that he should be replaced with a better 'disciple" or quality. There will always be twelve attributes, and when we spoke of the Twelve Disciples after the Crucifixion of Christ, it was with the thought of the replacement of this lower attribute with a higher or better one.

The Gospel According to
ST. JOHN

There is not much in this Gospel which we do not find in the previous ones. Nevertheless, there is some added illumination, and as we are desirous of giving our readers the benefit of every esoteric interpretation possible, we shall try to interpret the added light that St. John throws on the subject. St. John was the Beloved Disciple, and it is only natural that because of his unique standing, he should give a different viewpoint.

St. John begins with these words, "In the beginning was the WORD". The WORD, in one sense, is a state of vibration. It also refers to the second aspect of the Supreme Being. In the beginning of our Christian careers is the spiritual vibration or WORD, since this is the start of every Christian career. This can also be applied to a Masonic career, as the main purpose of Masonry is to recover the "lost word" or spiritual vibration that we once possessed. St. John tells us that the beginning of a Christian career starts with the finding of this "lost word" or high vibration which was lost when we committed the original sin and lowered our spiritual consciousness. In other words, we have lost the Christ vibration (in Masonry, "Hiram Abiff") that we once possessed when we dwelt in the spiritual worlds. When we have raised our vibrations until we are Christ-like, then we will find the "WORD" within. It is useless to look outwardly here and there in the world for the "lost word". It must be found within. As St. Paul says, the Christ must be formed within you.

This opening sentence of the Gospel of St. John may also apply to the beginning of a universe. In the beginning of actual manifestation is the WORD or Divine Fiat that sets the countless atoms of space to vibrating at a higher rate, until heat develops. When the heat becomes great enough, LIGHT comes into being. This is the real Cosmic Masonic LIGHT. "Let there be light".

So in the beginning of our occult or Christian careers must be the vibration of Christ or the WORD. John tells us that the "WORD was with GOD". This is logical, since the WORD is the vibration of one phase of God. St. John says the WORD *was* God. This is also evident, since we know it is the God Within.

"The same was in the beginning with God". This again in one sense, refers to the great Spirit which was with God in the beginning. In the personal sense, "As above so below". This indicates the second aspect of the Ego or Spirit Within.

"All things were made by him; and without him was not anything made that was made". Upon one plane of interpretation, this refers to the fact that the "word" or God Within made our bodies as they are now with the help of divine hierarchies. It indicates that nothing was made without the help of this second aspect of the Spirit. It also tells us that the universe was made by the divine WORD or second aspect of the Supreme Being. There are two distinct planes of interpretation in the above sentence by St. John. One is the work of the little "God" or the individual Spirit of each man and woman. The other is the work of the Supreme Being or Creator of all the solar systems.

"In him was life; and the life was the light of men. And the light shineth in darkness; and the darkness comprehended it not". The light of the being is the Spirit. It is also the life of the being. It is shining at present in the darkness of the material world and of the physical body. Both of these may be characterized as "darkness". The physical man and those deeply immersed in materiality certainly do not comprehend the things of the Spirit, and are therefore in spiritual darkness. It might also be said of the material world as a whole that it does not understand the "light" of the Spirit.

According to many interpreters, John the Baptist (the first human character mentioned by St. John) symbolizes the mind, which "must first come" and recognize the "Light". After the mind has done its work in the process of illumination, the heart (symbolized by the Christ) takes up the work and lives in and becomes the "Light". of the person and of the world. The heart shall some day be as much greater than the mind as Jesus Christ was greater than John. But at present the mind reigns supreme in a materialistic world. One might say of the material world that some slight echoes of John's teachings may have been heard, but the Christ has not yet come to the great majority, since they do not become the "Light" nor do they "walk in the Light".

The first story found in St. John which has not been related in the preceding Gospels is the miracle of turning of the water into wine at the Marriage of Cana. Christ and his Disciples were called to a marriage at Cana. When wine was requested, the mother of Jesus told Him of it. She requested the servants to do whatever He wished. Christ told the servants to fill six water pots with water. They filled the water pots to the brim. He then asked them to draw out and bear to the governor of the feast. When the governor of the feast tasted the water which had been made into wine, he did not know how it had happened. Those at the wedding told him it was unusual that he had kept the best wine until the last.

The six water pots symbolize the six ventricles of the brain. The servants represent different faculties within us, which the heart or emotional nature (represented by Jesus' mother) commands to obey the Christ Within. The governor of the feast symbolizes the mind. The water used is the "water of life", which is transformed from the lower use to the higher use as the "wine of life". This change is from the "water" of generation to the "wine" of regeneration. Wine is a mingled product and it is the mingling of the vibrations of the pineal gland and pituitary body which produces this spiritual "wine". Therefore this wedding feast signifies the "marriage" of the mind and the heart or the alchemical "wedding" within, in which clairvoyance or spiritual sight is produced.

Jesus told the Jews that if they destroyed the temple he would raise it up in three days. They thought He was referring to their place of worship. He meant that after three days (when the panorama of life is transferred to the higher vehicles after the death of the physical body), the Spirit will then raise up the "temple" or vehicle which has now become a spiritual "temple" instead of the physical which was destroyed. The real "temple" the spiritual "temple", cannot be harmed by our enemies.

Christ makes the statement to Nicodemus that, "Unless a man be born again, he cannot enter the kingdom of heaven". This has been interpreted many ways. The most important esoteric interpretation pertains to rebirth, wherein the Ego or Spirit incarnates in one body after another at intervals of approximately a thousand years, until it has learned all the lessons of life. Thus, it is plainly seen that unless a man be born again many times, he will not be qualified to enter into the kingdom of heaven. When an individual learns all of life's lessons, he becomes "a pillar in the house of God" and "comes in" and "goes out" no more. When an Ego has learned life's lessons it is no longer necessary to be born of woman. It will have reached such an advanced stage of evolution that it will possess the ability to perpetuate its physical body.

When Christ makes the statement that John was as great as any man that had been born of woman, we know that he (John) was a great Initiate, but still had not attained to Adeptship. An Adept no longer has to be born of woman in the physical world, as he can perpetuate his physical body. Therefore, John had not yet passed through the nine Lesser mysteries and the four Greater Mysteries. It is the attainment of the first of the Greater Mysteries which gives one the power to perpetuate the physical body.

The Gospel of St. John gives us an interesting story in the parable of Christ and the woman of Samaria at the well. This particular well is identified as the "Well of Jacob" or the spinal canal. The fact that Christ sat at the top of the well signifies that the Christ Force had been raised to the top of the spinal canal. Christ wishes a drink and asks the woman of Samaria to draw it for Him. This means that this Force must be continually drawn upward to "feed" the Christ Consciousness. We know that when we cease the process of "feeding" the Christ Within by raising the Force continually, we slip back again into our former condition of unholy living.

The woman of Samaria is surprised that the Christ, being a Jew, will drink water drawn by a Samaritan. The two types of people did not usually have any dealings with each other. A Jew, in this instance, represents the regenerate use of the Life Force. A Samaritan represents the physical use of the Life Force. However, Christ, in drinking the water drawn by the Samaritan woman, shows us that it is the same Force, which is at first used sensually, but is later purified and drawn upward to sustain the Christ Consciousness. This story teaches that the emotional nature must not cause the "water of life" to be used in sensuality, but must draw it upward in regeneration.

Christ tells the woman of Samaria that if she will drink of the water that He will give her, it will be a well of water springing up into everlasting life. In other words, if the emotional nature will use the Life Force only in the highest possible way, it will not only always satisfy her, but will produce eternal light and life.

It is interesting to note that this incident of Christ and the woman at the well took place at the sixth hour. This signifies that when the regenerative process takes place, the sixth sense, clairvoyance, will be developed. Christ tells the woman that she has no husband, although she has been married five times, This means that the feminine nature or the emotions have been "married" to the five physical senses, which is no true "marriage", but merely an animal existence. It is only when the "woman" within each of us is "wedded" to the God Within or the Spirit that we have a true spiritual "marriage".

Christ told the Disciples that they would reap where they had not sown. He said that the harvest was "white" and the laborers few. We know that others have preached and taught before us and have prepared our way. We also know that there is a crying need for teachers and speakers all over the country who will give the people real Christ truths. There are many teachers of a sort but few laborers of the Christ kind who have no will but to do the will of the Father, and who do not put material things before the things of the Spirit.

The story of the pool in Bethesda is an interesting one. There was a pool in Bethesda having five "porches". At intervals an angel came and troubled the water. The first person who stepped into the water after the angel had stirred it was made whole of whatever disease afflicted him: There was a certain man who had a disease of thirty-eight years, but was never able to be the first one to step into the pool. Someone else always got into the water before him. Christ cured the man and told him to go his way and sin no more lest a worse thing come upon him. The five porches of the pool represent the five physical senses, through which contacts with the physical world are made and our emotions aroused as a result of these contacts. Therefore, they are represented as five "porches" leading to the "pool" of the emotions, since it is through the five senses that the emotions are aroused. The angel who stirred the water is a higher spiritual force, which, while it is in our emotional nature, or when we have raised ourselves to this force emotionally, will cure any and all diseases. Thus, while our "pool of Bethesda" (within) is being troubled, or is in this higher vibration, our diseases gradnally disappear. But the man in the story could not get into the water soon enough. He had flashes of the higher emotional activity, but before he could derive any benefit from them, a physical emotion (another man) would step in before him or would usurp the place of the high emotion. This is the condition of the majority of us. We have a beautiful and lofty thought, but it does not last a second before a lower or material one has taken its place, and we have sunk back to our original position of waiting until another "angel" comes. However, when the Christ contacts us, He will cure our sins. He tells us, however, that if we do not cease committing the sin that caused the disease or limitation in the first place, it will come again upon us. This is one of God's laws, the Law of Cause and Effect. It decrees that we must reap as we sow. To be spiritual does not mean that we will always have health, etc. To maintain proper conditions always, we must always walk in harmony with the laws of God.

Christ states that the Father judges no man, but has committed all judgment unto the Son. Occult students know that this is scientifically true. The Christ principle in Man automatically, by way of the ethers, draws into his lungs with the air we breathe an exact picture of the vibrations surrounding us each moment of our lives. This is called the "breath record" and whether we realize it or not, there is recorded upon the seed atom in the heart the exact picture of each incident in our lives. When life is ended, the Spirit reviews the pictures in Purgatory concerning the undesirable parts of our lives, which are recorded in the force of this permanent atom. This is one phase of "hell", and is the "judgment" which the Life Spirit or the Christ principle in Man has charge of in our evolution.

In the First Heaven the Spirit reviews the good acts of the life and experiences as much joy at this time as it did sorrow over the sins committed.

Christ says the "dead" shall hear the word of God. It is the belief of the writer that He refers to those who are "dead" spiritually. We know that those who pass on gradually eliminate their material phases of being and come closer to the "word" of God. Therefore, this saying works two ways. There will also come a time when the spiritually "dead" shall awaken to the spiritual life. We shall each of us in time "die daily" to the things of the lower man.

We are told by Christ that He can do nothing of Himself, but that it is the Father working in Him. We are taught in occult work that it is the power of the Absolute or First Cause that is "stepped down" through our Triune God. This is done so that we may utilize this force without fear of being destroyed, as might be the case if it were not thus transformed or lessened. Naturally, it would be impossible for either the Christ or the Holy Ghost to function without this power which comes from the Father principle, just as it would also be impossible for the Father to function if it were not for a still higher power which flows from still another phase of the Spiritual principle. The chain is endless. There is a God of our solar system and there is the God of all solar systems.

We are told that Moses shall accuse us before God. Moses represents the Jehovistic Law, the Law of Karma. The accusation referred to is the record which will show where we have violated or gone contrary to this great Law. There is no escape from it. Our debts must be paid, either willingly in service or unwilling as Karma.

The Jews are told by Christ that unless they eat of His flesh and drink of His blood they have no life. This they are unable to understand. The explanation is this: At the Crucifixion the great Christ Spirit entered into the aura of the earth. Once each year He enters completely into the earth, and fructifies all the tiny seeds which go to make up the food we eat. Consequently, in a sense, whenever we eat or drink, we are eating and drinking the "body" and "blood" of Christ, since His life is in the food.

We wish to explain the statement, at this time, that we are all made of "dust". We are not literally made of dust. However, as the mineral elements in the soil nourish the plants and we eat the plants in order to live, our atoms are renewed in this way indirectly by the minerals of the soil. Thus it might be said, in one sense, that we are made of, or maintained by, "dust" or the mineral kingdom.

"He that believeth on me—out of his belly shall flow rivers of living water". The interpretation of this truth given out by the Christ is as follows: When we become regenerated, the Life Force, symbolically known as the "river of life", shall ascend from the lower being (the "belly") to the head, bringing illumination and lighting the "candle" of the "churches" described in Revelation. Thus, from the true Christian the "water of life" shall flow from his "belly", bringing liberation from the cross of the body and making him a true "Master Mason".

A story found exclusively in St. John is that of the woman taken in adultery. A woman is brought to the Christ who had been taken in the very act of adultery. Those who seized her quoted Moses as saying that she should be stoned. They ask Christ what should be done to her. This incident was supposed to have taken place in the temple. The scribes and Pharisees represent phases of the mind. The woman of course represents the heart. It has been guilty of violating a law and the mental attributes pass harsh judgment on it, as they are capable of seeing only the letter of the law. But Christ, with the Love-Wisdom which He brings into the "temple" of the being, sees only with the eyes of love. He refuses to listen to the things which the scribes and Pharisees tell Him about the woman. This fact has a very deep occult significance. The Christ Consciousness in Man will have nothing to do with evil thoughts and treats them with indifference. Indifference is the only weapon with which to fight these things. The only way in which we may prove that we have conquered evil is by being indifferent to it in a personal sense. Christ radiated the love vibration, which automatically overcomes the vibration of sin.

Christ realizes that almost all evil originated in the mind, since the mind was formed from one half of our original sexual powers. He also knows that if the scribes and Pharisees were not so intensely interested in evil, they would not be so eager to criticize the fallen woman. Therefore, when He wrote on the ground, "Let him that is without sin cast the first stone", not one of the scribes or Pharisees was able to accuse the woman.

The mind blames all of its troubles and downfalls on the emotional nature. The Christ Wisdom shows us this is not correct. In this symbolic story we are taught that if the mind were clean, it would not condemn the heart, since evil is more attached to the mental phase of being than to the heart. Remember the Bible statement, "The imagination of man is evil from his youth". Youth here refers to the period of puberty or the beginning of the manifestation of sex. Therefore, we must not, as the scribes and Pharisees, lay the blame for our sins on the "woman" or emotional self, but must get at the source of it in the mind. When we do this, we shall find that the heart will do as Christ told the fallen woman. "Go and sin no more". The heart will no longer sin when it is under the influence of the Christ, but the Christ cannot rule Man until the mind is first cleansed.

It is said that Mary Magdalene was a fallen woman. She became one of the greatest of the saints. "The greater the sinner, the greater the saint", is an occult maxim. Let us therefore not condemn others who are learning lessons, though perhaps not the same ones as ourselves at the same time.

"Then Jesus said unto them, When ye have lifted up the Son of man, then shall ye know that I am he, and that I do nothing of myself; but as my Father has taught me, I speak these things".

This verse has a twofold significance. When the Christ had been lifted up and crucified, the people realized afterwards that He was the Christ, as He had told them. Individually, when we "lift up" the Christ Force within by way of the spinal canal to "the place of the skull" in our own bodies, we shall know that of ourselves we can do nothing. We shall also come to know and understand the Christ Force which works within, and also the Father principle from which the Christ Force comes.

Christ tells the Jews who believe, that if they continue in His word, they are His disciples indeed. Remember that the symbolic meaning of a Jew is one who has been circumcised spiritually or who has sacrificed the lower use of the flesh. A "word" is a vibration, and the "word" of Christ is the vibration of Christ. It is indeed true that if we continue in this vibration or on this high spiritual level, we shall in very truth be the "disciples" of Christ.

Our next story is the healing of a blind man by the Christ. This story brings out different points, both physically and spiritually, from other accounts of Christ's healing of the blind. In the present incident the Disciples ask, "Master, who did sin, this man or his parents, that he was born blind. Christ answers, "Neither hath this man sinned, nor his parents: but that the works of God should be made manifest in him". This clearly illustrates the Law of Cause and Effect, which governs all acts of life. Christ tells us that the parents had not sinned. If sins of parents were visited upon their helpless children, there would be no justice in life. Elsewhere in the Bible it states that sins of the parents are visited upon the children to the third and fourth generation. This is merely referring to physical heredity. The occult student knows that there is a still higher law back of the law of physical heredity, which decrees that only those Egos who merit physical defects will be born to parents who are able to handicap them with these physical defects.

In our present case, the Christ plainly brings out that it is not our parents who are responsible for our physical shortcomings, but that we get in life exactly what we have earned in the school of evolution. The working of this law may be seen in cases where great men have rather ordinary children and brilliant-minded men have idiot sons, etc.

Christ also said that this man had not sinned who was born blind. Naturally so, since he was born blind before he had a chance to sin in this life. Then Christ gives us the real explanation in His words, "that the works (or law) of God should be made manifest in him". It might also be expressed, "that the works of (the) God should be made manifest in him". In other words, the Ego or "God" within this man had violated some Cosmic law in a previous life so that when he was born again, he was forced to go through the suffering of blindness until the law of God, which he had violated, should become manifest. When he had thoroughly learned this law he would no longer violate it in the future. (Many times the physical man does not realize the cause of the limitations under which he is suffering. Nevertheless, the Ego or Spirit will learn when it has violated God's laws in this way).

It is interesting to note that the Christ only healed this man after he had been blind for some time. Otherwise, the lesson might not have been learned. This is food for thought which we might all meditate upon. Many of us would like certain limitations removed from our lives. They can only be removed when we have learned the lessons in connection with them and understand the reason for their having been imposed upon us. Then our "eyes" shall be opened and we will "go and sin no more".

The blind man was told to go and wash his eyes. Each of us must "wash our eyes" in the "River Jordan" or "river of life" that flows up the spinal canal to the "All-seeing Eye" in the head. When this "eye" is washed in this spiritual stream it becomes "open" and able to "see".

"And Jesus said, For judgment I am come into this world, that they which see not might see; and that they which see might be made blind. And some of the Pharisees which were with him heard these words, and said unto him, Are we blind also? Jesus said unto them, If ye were blind, ye should have no sin: but now ye say, We see; therefore your sin remaineth".

The meaning of these verses is that when we do not understand a certain law of God, there is no sin on our part when we violate this law. This does not mean, however, that we shall not have to pay for the violation. It simply means that there is no conscious sin on our part. But when we say we "see", as did the Pharisees, it means that we know this law, and therefore it is a sin if we violate it. A child does wrong unknowingly and it is no sin. The meaning of the words, "they which see might be made blind", is that those who understand spiritually might be "blinded" to the lusts of the world or be made immune to them.

"Verily, verily, I say unto you. He that entereth not by the door into the sheepfold, but climbeth up some other way, the same is a thief and a robber. But he that entereth in by the door is the shepherd of the sheep. To him the porter openeth; and the sheep hear his voice; and he calleth his own sheep by name, and leadeth them out. And when he putteth forth his own sheep, he goeth before them, and the sheep follow him: for they know his voice. And a stranger will they not follow, but will flee from him: for they know not the voice of strangers".

Christ here represents the shepherd. The door into the sheepfold is "opened" by following His teachings and the symbolic story of His life step by step. Anyone who enters into the "sheepfold" or the other planes of consciousness by any other method is the black magician, who leaves his body a "lower" way instead of through the head. The "sheep" know the "voice" or vibration of the Christ and they follow Him or aspire to live the Christ life. They will not follow a false light or a "stranger" after they have seen and felt the true light of Christ.

The story of the raising of Lazarus from the dead by the Christ is a story of Initiation. Christ was the Initiator. Lazarus his friend, whom He loved, had made himself ready to be "raised" to a high degree of Initiation. That is why Lazarus was said to have been "dead" for three days. Christ says distinctly, however, that the "sickness of Lazarus was not unto death but for the glory of God, that the Son of God might be glorified thereby". This is generally taken to mean that this miracle was performed so that the Christ could exhibit His powers. This was true, but the statement refers to the Christ principle within Lazarus. Jesus Christ, the actual person, had no wish to perform a miracle merely to show off His powers.

Christ did not go to Lazarus immediately. Lazarus was out of his body and was to be raised by Christ at the proper time. The true significance of this incident is that Lazarus lay "bound" in the "grave" of materiality in the "grave clothes" or those things which hold one to the lower planes. Christ caused Lazarus, with the sound of His voice or with His vibration, to come forth from the "grave" of materiality and be "loosed" from the "clothes" that bound him. The esoteric student who knows of a certain "cloth" which has to be "loosened" at a certain stage of our development, please meditate upon this.

The next story contains much for the esoteric student to ponder over. It is the story in which Christ was eating with His Disciples and Mary annointed His feet with precious ointment. This act of annointing the feet symbolizes the awakening of the spiritual centers in the feet. This is done by directing the Life Force, which is here represented by Mary's annointing the Christ's feet with the ointment, to this part of the body. Mary represents the emotional nature which formerly had been a "fallen woman" or had wasted the Life Force, but now had accepted the Christ. When this Life Force is no longer wasted, it becomes a "precious ointment", which "annoints" the feet and other spiritual centers of the body.

The fact that Judas complained at the expenditure of this ointment might be the subject for much meditation. He was described as "a thief" and he carried the "silver" in the "bag". The lower nature is always betraying us, and the reason for Judas' complaint was that he, the lower nature, wished to utilize the value or power of this "ointment" for his own evil ends. The story makes it appear that Judas wished to sell the ointment and give the money to the poor. This was merely an excuse of the lower nature to veil his real purpose.

Much interesting information is brought out in the incident of the washing of the Disciples' feet by the Christ, especially concerning the conversation between Christ and St. Peter. The washing of the feet symbolizes, for one thing, the humility that is required of the Initiate. For another, it represents the cleansing of the spiritual centers in the feet by the Christ Force.

When St. Peter asks the Christ to wash his hands and head also, we are given the location of the other spiritual centers of the vital body. These also must in time be purified by the Christ Force. Possibly the reason that Christ replied to Peter that when his feet were washed, he would be entirely clean is that the centers in the feet are probably the last to be set into activity. When they have been made active, the person will very likely be entirely purified. This story also symbolizes the fact that the Teacher must advance to greater heights through service to those of a lesser degree of attainment. It is through "loving, self-forgetting service" that we advance in the kingdom of God.

The promise of Christ to send the Holy Ghost, may indicate the great work He has done for us, "from that place where he went", in purifying the earth's desire body and helping us to control the animal within. The Holy Ghost has His counterpart in the Triune God within as the Human Spirit. Its lower octave is the desire body. It is the cleansing of the desire body which marks the first real step on the occult path. Part of the greatest work which Christ did was to cleanse the planetary desire body of the earth. This made it possible for us to secure purer material for our own individual desire bodies. Thus did Christ send the Holy Ghost to humanity in the form of its greater influence in the three-fold Ego through its purer vehicles in which to influence the physical man.

The question of Pilate, "What is truth'", can be the subject of much meditation. The "Cosmo-Conception" says that "Truth is eternal and the search for truth must also be eternal. Truth cannot be once and for all delivered". As our consciousness expands, our conception of Truth will also expand. Therefore, there cannot be the same exact idea concerning the truth of a thing to any two persons. It is only when we are able to raise our consciousness to the level of the Christ Consciousness that we are able to perceive and know what Truth is.

Christ appeared to the Disciples after the Crucifixion when they had been fishing all night, but had caught nothing. He told them to cast the net on the right side of the ship. When they did so they were not able to draw it in because it was weighed down with fish. One esoteric interpretation is this. We, as "fishers of men", trying to raise our brothers to a purer life from the low regions of the "sea of passion" will only be successful when we "cast our nets" from the "right" or positive side of the "ship". Spiritual development that comes with the "left" or negative side of being is dangerous for all students. In the opinion of the writer, those who use ouija boards, consult mediums, attend seances or use automatic writing are disobeying the command of the Christ to "fish" from the "right side" of the "ship" or the body.

When Peter casts himself into the sea, it is symbolical of the fact that he went to the Christ on the spiritual plane in which He functioned. A better way to state Peter's act is to say that he went to Christ *above* the "sea", since the sea represents the Desire World and Christ was functioning on a much higher plane. The three commands given to Peter by the Christ, "Feed my lambs. Feed my sheep", and again, "Feed my sheep", refer to the three stages of advancement through which each neophyte must pass or be "fed". In Masonry there are also three steps to Master Masonship. There are also three steps in the Rosicrucian school.

The Beloved Disciple, John, symbolizes LOVE. The fact that he tarried until Christ came, indicates that it is through love that we can bring the Christ into our lives. If we culivate the love principle represented by John, we will not have to "tarry" very long until the Christ will be a living factor in our lives. It is the prayer of the writer that we may all become "John" and radiate the love that will bring the Christ and His teachings into our lives as a living thing; that the Christ will be born in the "manger" of our bodies and raised to the "Jerusalem" within; that He will be "liberated" and in turn liberate us from the "cross" of the body. We pray that He will ascend to the "Father" within and bring down the Holy Ghost to us, so that we may "speak with tongues", as did St. Germaine, that we may heal the sick, raise the dead (from spiritual death to spiritual life) and preach the gospel of glad tidings to all the world, so that the kingdom of Christ may actually come to the earth. Then we shall each live under "his own vine and fig tree" and none shall make us afraid. This is the sincere prayer of the writer, and he hopes that the reader will be helped to cooperate in this, as a result of some little light that he may glean from these pages.

NOTE: The thought occurred to the writer that the reader may not perfectly understand some of the statements Christ made concerning His relationship, etc. to the Father. The Father Within is the invisible Father Fire which is above the "mercy seat" in the "dome" or "west room" of our temple, the body. Naturally, the Christ Within, the "Flame", comes from the Father Within or the "Invisible Fire", since the Christ is a manifestation of that Fire. To know the "Christ" (the "Flame") would be to know the "Father" (the Invisible Fire) from which comes the "Flame". That is why Christ said that no man "cometh unto the Father" except through Him. He said also that He went to the Father, etc. When all of these statements are analyzed in the relationship of the Christ Light or Flame to the invisible Father Fire, they become perfectly clear. When the "Christ" has ascended to the

"Father" or "Father Fire" in the "dome" of the "temple" or body, the invisible fire manifests as a light or flame. Then indeed do we know that Christ and the Father are one.

We would like to close this book with a prayer. The most complete prayer given to mankind is the "Lord's Prayer". It is all-embracing and takes in our every need, both physically and spiritually. Since the "Lord's Prayer", however, is fully explained in the "Rosicrucian Cosmo-Conception", we will not use it here. Instead we will use the "Twenty-third Psalm".

"The Lord is my shepherd". Sheep symbolizes Purity, and it is the "Lord" or God Within who "keeps our sheep" or preserves our purity.

"I shall not want". This "want" refers to spiritual as well as material needs. If we live and pray aright we shall never want, since "all things are added to those who do all things as unto the Lord".

"He maketh me to lie down in green pastures". Green is a blending of yellow (or gold) and blue, which are the colors of the Christ and His Father. Thus we are fed on the spiritual food of Devotion (the Father) and Love-Wisdom (the Christ).

"He leadeth me beside the still waters". Water represents the emotional nature, and we are told in this verse that the God Within will still the turbulent "storms" of unlawful emotions and will bring to us perfect peace and spiritual joy.

"He restoreth my soul". It is the Spirit or God Within alone who can restore the soul, after the lower self has degraded it through sin against God's laws. As the carnal life is "death", so the spiritual life is "life everlasting".

"He leadeth me in the paths of righteousness for his Name's sake". A name is a vibration, and we know that if we follow or live in the vibration of God's holy Name, we will be led into a beautiful and righteous life.

"Yea, though I walk through the valley of the shadow of death, I will fear no evil for thou art with me; thy rod and thy staff they comfort me". The "valley of the shadow of death" may refer to the actual condition that we call death. It may also refer to Initiation, in which the candidate crosses over consciously onto the planes where dwell the so-called "dead". When we reach such a point in our spiritual careers, we shall have no fear because the God Within will light the way. The "rod" and the "staff" symbolize the spinal canal or "Aaron's rod" which "buds". When the spinal canal or "vine" buds, or the Life Force ascends to the "dome of the temple", we will have light, and for us there will be no more "darkness". We shall stand in the presence of the God Within, and therefore shall have no fear.

"Thou preparest a table before me in the presence of mine enemies". The "table" which the God Within prepares for us is the one whereon the spiritual feast is spread for those who have regenerated themselves and developed positive clairvoyance and clairaudience. The "feast" which they will enjoy will be the privilege of gazing into the heaven worlds. They will see the beauty of the celestial realms and hear the heavenly melodies. The "enemies" that the "feast" is prepared in the presence of are the lower attributes of being, who will not be able to partake of this "feast". Neither will they be allowed to spoil the "feast" by using the Life Force in a way that would ultimately bring death.

"Thou annointest my head with oil". This "oil" is the same as that explained by Proffessor Smiley on Page 20 of "Revelation, Esoterically Interpreted" by the writer. This is the oil which is secreted into the blood stream by the cardia in the process of regeneration. When this oil flows through the blood stream and "annoints" the body in sufficient force, we will be able to do all of the things which the Bible says a true Christian can do, among which is the ability to drink poison and be bitten by poisonous reptiles with no ill effects. This oil is the "virgin oil" which lights the "lamp" of the being. This "lamp", however, is no mere figment of the imagination. It is the "all-seeing eye" and gives an actual light which floods the "temple" of the being.

"My cup runneth over". This refers to the "sacrament cup" of the body in the sacral region. It is necessary that we fill this "cup" and "run it over" before the beautiful things mentioned above can happen to us. This is the "cup" that holds the "blood of the Christ" and the "wine of life" spoken of by Omar Khayyam.

"Surely goodness and mercy shall follow me all the days of my life; and I will dwell in the house of the Lord forever". The individual who accomplishes the results described above will, indeed, dwell in the "house of the Lord". His body will become a temple sacred to God, and his consciousness will be that of the heaven worlds. Goodness and mercy, two qualities which go with such a development, will be his companions, both radiating from him and returning to him, forever and ever. He will enjoy the perfect peace that "passes all understanding" and that spiritual love enjoyed by one who is "beloved of God". May we all some day attain to this, -

and

MAY THE ROSES BLOOM UPON YOUR CROSS